Circular Economy - Recent Advances, New Perspectives and Applications

Edited by Tao Zhang

Published in London, United Kingdom

IntechOpen

Supporting open minds since 2005

Circular Economy - Recent Advances, New Perspectives and Applications
http://dx.doi.org/10.5772/intechopen.90982
Edited by Tao Zhang

Contributors
Hanim Kamaruddin, Rosilah Hassan, Norasmah Othman, Wan Mimi Diyana Bt Zaki, Sarmila Md Sum, Oleg Golichenko, Smitha Chandran, Razim Mohammed S, Rossitsa Chobanova, Virginia Ivanova Zhelyazkova, Jean Pierre Doussoulin, Librita Arifiani, Harjanto Prabowo, Asnan Furinto, Wibowo Kosasih

First published in London, United Kingdom, 2021 by IntechOpen
IntechOpen is the global imprint of INTECHOPEN LIMITED, registered in England and Wales, registration number: 11086078, 5 Princes Gate Court, London, SW7 2QJ, United Kingdom
Printed in Croatia

British Library Cataloguing-in-Publication Data
A catalogue record for this book is available from the British Library

Additional hard and PDF copies can be obtained from orders@intechopen.com

Circular Economy - Recent Advances, New Perspectives and Applications
Edited by Tao Zhang
p. cm.
Print ISBN 978-1-83880-166-3
Online ISBN 978-1-83881-070-2
eBook (PDF) ISBN 978-1-83881-071-9

For EU product safety concerns:
IN TECH d.o.o., Prolaz Marije Krucifikse Kozulić 3, 51000 Rijeka, Croatia, info@intechopen.com or visit our website at intechopen.com.

Meet the editor

Tao Zhang completed his Ph.D. from Nanjing University. He is an Associate Professor, Ph.D. supervisor, and the Deputy Dean of the Department of Environment Science and Engineering, College of Resources and Environmental Sciences, China Agricultural University. He was a visiting scholar at Arizona State University in 2014 and in the University of Hohenheim in 2017. He has published 60 papers in highly reputed international journals, such as Chemical Engineering Journal, Water Research, Green Chemistry, Journal of Hazardous Materials, Bioresource Technology, and Science of the Total Environment, and has been authorized 17 China invention patents. He has won the prize "Science Chinese for Outstanding Young Scientist".

Contents

Preface

With the rapid development of the economy, human civilization has experienced fishing and hunting civilization, as well as agricultural civilization to the present green civilization. The relationship between the economy and environment has also changed from pursuing economic growth at the expense of the environment to the harmonious development of the economy and environment. Cleaner production and a circular economy have become the general trend of global development.

How to adjust the relationship between resources, ecological environment, and economic development and protect the environment in promoting economic growth has become a major goal pursued by producers. The purpose of this book is to provide a comprehensive overview for reading, deepen everyone's understanding of a circular economy, change the original way of thinking and lifestyle, and promote the development of society towards a virtuous circle.

Tao Zhang
China Agricultural University,
Beijing, China

Section 1

Practice Circular Economy and Take the Road of Green Development

Chapter 1

Circular Economy as a New Stage of Economic Development

Rossitsa Chobanova

Abstract

The chapter is devoted to understanding circular economy as a new stage of economic development, which is aimed to respect limited quantity of water, soil, clean air and ecosystem services, strongly connected to the new global social tensions, and how to achieve this stage. The literature survey has shown the current concepts for circular economy discuss new usage of resources, but not who and how will provide such changes. That is why it is suggested application of the Hegelian doctrine for economic development which is answering similar (we mean social) to the above questions – how to get freedom and society consolidation in market economy, suggesting state regulation of market economy. Consequently such regulation is needed to overcome the social tensions strongly connected to limited quantity of resources, vital for the future of society. Taking this doctrine as a theoretical background, it is assumed each new stage of economic development is characterised by different content of goals, subject and means for achieving the goals. The applicability of the notion circular economy is a new stage of economic development is tested and approved by demonstrated contemporary changes in policies for economic development, taking place in the European union, by recently changed and achieved goals of its development.

Keywords: circular economy, economic development, Hegel, theory, measure

1. Introduction

The recent tensions in the globalised world are strongly connected to resources in limited quantities. In this regard, the importance of producing more value using less material and diversifying consumption has been become a driver for developing variety of concepts of circular economy. The chapter is aimed at:

- summarising the recent achievements in understanding economic development and circularity of resources presented in these concepts;
- identifying understandings how and who will transform linear free market economy into a circular one;
- defining a theoretical background to solve the above problems;
- approbating its applicability into the practice.

2. Understanding the economic development and circularity

Economic development is a term in which different content is invested. Based on etymology, it means a constant process of transition of the state of the economy from one stage to another more advanced one. In the scientific literature many different classifications of the stages of economic development and respected criteria for their identification take place. Practically none of them discusses circularity as a criterion for belonging to a specific stage. For this study we accept the main characteristic of the recent stage of economy development is that it is a free market one, and that the main challenges before is digitalization and circularity implementation. The latter is the focus of the further analyses.

2.1 Circular economy concepts

The basic concept of a circular economy depicts a production and consumption system that relies on the recycling, re-use, repair, remanufacturing, sharing of products, changing the consumption patterns and new business models and systems. Defining circular economy concepts and their problems could be find in academic literature, including contemporary academic reviews, official documents of the European Commission [1], OECD, G-8, etc., and from charities and NGOs, most prominently, the Ellen McArthur Foundation [2].

Contemporary academic rethinking of the progress within the limits of the planet has contributed to development of different theoretical and methodological dimensions of a concept for circular economy and for a transition from linear to a circular economy [3, 4]. They have concerned also measurement of the change like to redefine growth, focusing on society – wide benefits. The concept of circularity transforms all the elements of the take-make-waste system how to manage resources, how to make and use products, and what is done with the materials afterwards in the process of transforming linear to circular economy. (See: **Figure 1**).

Another dimension of concepts on the circular economy identified is focussed on how materials enter, flow within and (eventually) leave the economy. A visual overview is provided by a material flows diagram (See **Figure 2**[1]). It shows all raw materials — aggregated as well as grouped by categories of materials — throughout the economy, from their extraction until they become waste.

More concretely, the input-side on the left shows that only 0.6 billion of 8 billion tonnes of materials are processed into energy or products annually in the EU originate from recycling. On the output-side, out of the 2.2 billion tonnes of waste that are generated only 0.6 billion tonnes re-enter the system as recycled materials. It means that the rest of the materials, equivalent to 1.5 billion tonnes, is waste. This concept for circular economy points to a significant potential for improvement in particular by increasing the share of materials recycled as secondary raw materials and decreasing the production of waste.

It could be assumed the above two dimensions of concepts for circular economy discuss how resources are used, or have to be used. But they do not characterise who and how will transform the linear free market economy to a circular one. Such answer could be found applying the Hegelian doctrine for economic development.

2.2 Hegelian economic development doctrine

The most of the recent conflicts are originating from the limited quantities of resources such as water, soil, clean air and ecosystem services which are vital to health and quality of life, but also to the human society as such.

[1] Energetic use covers raw materials used for combustion or production of food and feed.

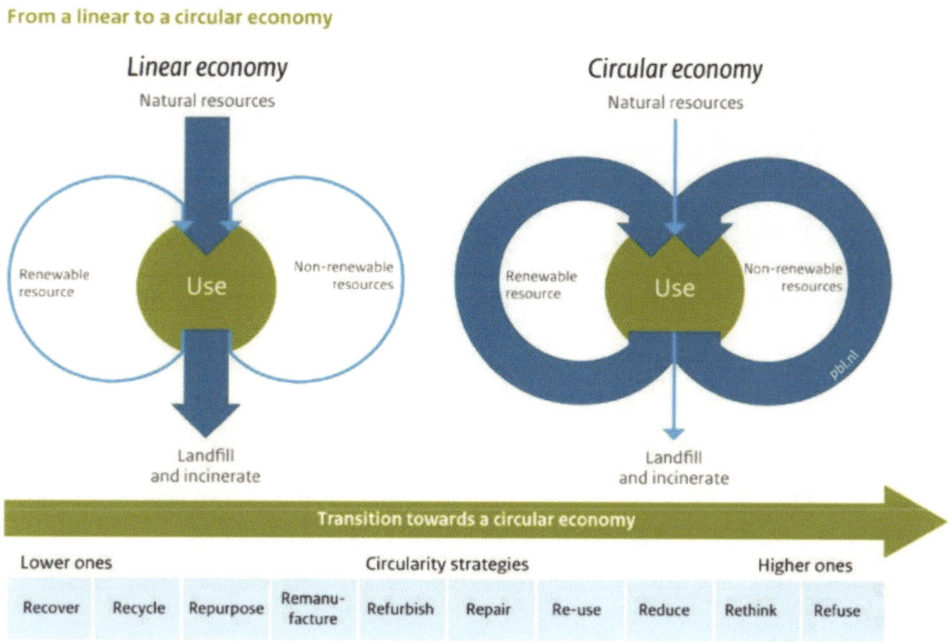

Figure 1.
From linear to circular economy. Source: [5].

In all of this Hegel appears to be providing a philosophical account of modern economic developments[2]. He argues the economy, especially through the division of labor, produces fragmentation and diminishment of human life and the state must not only address social problems but also provide the means for the people's political participation to further the development of social self-consciousness. Regarding to it the state must not only address this phenomenon but also provide the means for the people's political participation to further the development of social self-consciousness. Such participation could be understood as defining and introducing the objectives and means for economic development. Hegel repeats the need for strong state regulation of the economy, which if left to its own workings is blind to the needs of the social community.

Since start of Industrial revolution, the Hegelian doctrine for economic development has become more attractive in the frame of the concept for forth industrial revolution. It is because the notion the free market economy without a state does not contribute to meeting challenges such as diminishing freedom and fragmentation of social community is still correct now-a-days. Today the Hegelian doctrine is attractive also for understanding and approaching the challenges before health and life of human beings, which affect freedom and social community fragmentation also. This doctrine suggests an answer to the question how to avoid the negative effects of traditional linear economy, where raw materials are used to make a product, and after its use any waste (e.g. packaging) is thrown away. Here we are not discussing the level of which a state is able to meet such expectations.

[2] The core of Hegel's social and political thought are the concepts of freedom, reason, self-consciousness, and recognition. Regarding economic development, although Hegel provides a defence of modern market societies, he calls into question their corrosive effects on society as a whole. The thoughts for economic development could be find in the manuscripts entitled *Realphilosophie*, based on lectures Hegel delivered at Jena University in 1803–04 (*Realphilosophie I*) and 1805–06 (*Realphilosophie II*), and were originally published by Johannes Hoffmeister in 1932.

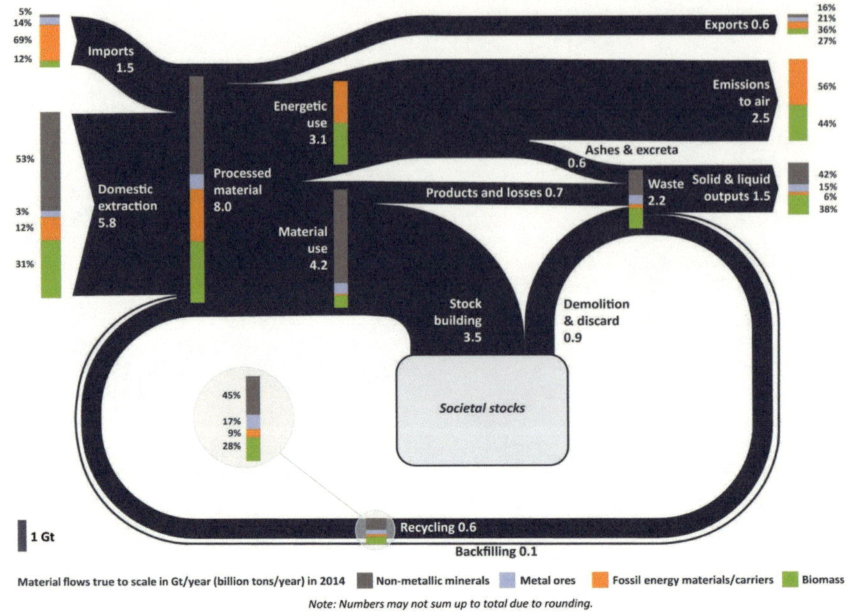

Figure 2.
Material flows in the economy (EU-28, 2014). *Source: [6].*

It could be assumed in regard to economic development the Hegel's theory [7] respects criteria for identification of different stages of this development - the object (goal), the subject (state) and the means for achieving the goals (free market vs., or with state regulation). If this assumption is correct we could conclude the circular economy is a stage of economic development, where circularity of resources is important integral part of the goal of the economic development. The achievement the goal of circularity, understood as minimising the usage of natural resources, minimised or 0 waste needs strong state monitoring and regulation in the frame of a free market economy.

3. Monitoring circular economic development

Monitoring circular economy is of vital importance for the society. It will be analysed on the case of European union. The monitoring there is based on identification of main areas of appearance of circularity and defining the available indicators to measure them. This approach has allowed monitoring assessment, strategy development and policy making and implementation. As such areas of circularity appearance identified are:

- Sustainable resource management;
- Societal behaviour;
- Business operations.

The content of indicators and interpretation of their contribution to understanding of circular economy is grouped according to the areas of circularity appearance as follow [8]:

SUSTAINABLE RESOURCE MANAGEMENT - indicators examining the performance of the EU Member States in transforming their economies toward circularity by lowering resource demands, thereby increasing resource security and lowering pressures on the environment domestically and abroad.

SOCIETAL BEHAVIOUR – indicators, reflecting citizen awareness, engagement and participation in the circular economy. Citizen engagement, behaviour change and social norms are integral to the success of a circular economy transition. This means that people participate in new forms of consumption (e.g. sharing, product-service systems, willingness to pay more for durability), re-use (requiring changed mindsets regarding repair and refurbishment), and disposal (separating waste streams and bringing "waste" to remanufacturing/ recycling/ sorting sites).

BUSINESS OPERATIONS – indicators, which depict eco-innovation activities toward changing and adapting business models according to the principles of a circular economy. Business activities and their digitalization are the engine behind the circular economy transition. They foster circularity across the life-cycle of material use, beginning with how and what materials are sourced (quality, environmental and health standards). The design stage of business operations is particularly crucial to enabling re-use /re-manufacturing / recycling and raising the durability of goods for keeping within the economy longer. Remanufacturing and recycling are key business operations critical to scaling up the circular economy.

The monitoring and assessment of circularity have become a fundament for developing vast majority of economic development policy measures.

4. Circular economy development policy measures in Europe

The transition to a more circular economy in Europe is accompanied by implementation of several specific policy measures.

In 2015 the EC adopted an action plan to accelerate Europe's transition to a circular economy. It was aimed at strengthen global competitiveness, promote sustainable economic growth and create new jobs. This action plan contains 54 measures to "close the loop" of the life cycle of products - from production and consumption to waste management and the market for secondary raw materials. Five priority sectors to accelerate the transition along the value chain are identified: plastics, food waste, critical raw materials, construction and demolition, biomass and bio-based materials.

The strategic documents of today EU institutions include:

- A clear resource efficiency agenda;
- Roadmap to a resource efficient Europe;
- The Circular Economy package;
- Amendments to renewable energy policy that seek to address resource issues.

The transition to a circular economy is in the agenda of world fora as well. It was in the focus of discussions during the 2019 Annual Meeting in Davos. The four key priorities emerging for the year ahead identified are as follow:

a. Leadership is critical;

b. Leverage the potential of the Fourth Industrial Revolution;

c. Circular material value chains;

d. Collaboration is key.

Implementation of the developed visions, strategies and respective policy measures has required developing respective instruments. On the first place they concern defining appropriate indicators.

5. Circularity: indicators for assessing economic development policy implementation

The literature suggests different methodologies to be applied for collecting and interpreting data for monitoring and assessing policy measures for circular economy. There are a variety of indicators applied now, although most have limitations. There are two most used indicators, predominantly applied by the OECD and G-8, more concretely those:

- for resource productivity and
- for resource efficiency.

The first indicator is measuring circularity as a ratio between GDP and domestic material consumption, in other words, it is focusing circularity on the resource use.

The second one means using the Earth's limited resources in a sustainable manner while minimising impacts on the environment. It allows interpreting the level of creating more with less and to deliver greater value with less input. Such indicator is also measured through EU resource efficiency scoreboard [9], as EU eco-innovation index recycling rates [10, 11], through the amount of municipal waste per capita, or amount of waste per GDP output.

The monitoring framework on the circular economy as set up by the European Commission consists of ten indicators, some of which are broken down in sub-indicators, selected in order to capture the main elements of a circular economy. These ten indicators are divided into four thematic areas [8]:

Production and consumption. This area comprises four indicators:

- Self-sufficiency of raw materials for production in the EU;
- Green public procurement (as an indicator for financing aspects);
- Waste generation (as an indicator for consumption aspects);
- Food waste.

Waste management. This area comprises two indicators:

- Recycling rates (the share of waste which is recycled);
- Specific waste streams (packaging waste, bio-waste, e-waste, etc.).

Secondary raw materials. This area comprises two indicators:

- Contribution of recycled materials to raw materials demand;
- Trade of recyclable raw materials between the EU Member States and with the rest of the world.

Competitiveness and innovation. This area comprises two indicators:

- Private investments, jobs and gross value added;
- Patents related to recycling and secondary raw materials as a proxy for innovation.

This European monitoring framework aims at measuring progress toward a circular economy in a way that encompasses its various dimensions at all stages of the lifecycle of resources, products and services. In this regard the monitoring framework has a set of the ten indicators (see **Table 1**), grouped into four stages and aspects of the circular economy: (1) production and consumption, (2) waste management, (3) secondary raw materials and (4) competitiveness and innovation. The logic and structure of this monitoring framework broadly follows the logic and structure of the European circular economy action plan.

Production and consumption			
1	EU self-sufficiency for raw materials	The circular economy should help to address the supply risks for raw materials, in particular critical raw materials.	Raw Materials Initiative; Resource Efficiency Roadmap
2	Green public procurement*	Public procurement accounts for a large share of consumption and can drive the circular economy.	Public Procurement Strategy; EU support schemes and voluntary criteria for green public procurement
3a-c	Waste generation	In a circular economy waste generation is minimised.	Waste Framework Directive; directives on specific waste streams; Strategy for Plastics
4	Food waste*	Discarding food has negative environmental, climate and economic impacts.	General Food Law Regulation; Waste Framework Directive; various initiatives (e.g. Platform on Food Losses and Food Waste)
Waste management			
5a-b	Overall recycling rates	Increasing recycling is part of the transition to a circular economy.	Waste Framework Directive
6a-f	Recycling rates for specific waste streams	This reflects the progress in recycling key waste streams.	Waste Framework Directive; Landfill Directive; directives on specific waste streams

Secondary raw materials			
7a-b	Contribution of recycled materials to raw materials demand	In a circular economy, secondary raw materials are commonly used to make new products.	Waste Framework Directive; Eco-design Directive; EU Ecolabel; REACH; initiative on the interface between chemicals, products and waste policies; Strategy for Plastics; quality standards for secondary raw materials
8	Trade in recyclable raw materials	Trade in recyclables reflects the importance of the internal market and global participation in the circular economy.	Internal Market policy; Waste Shipment Regulation; Trade policy
Competitiveness and innovation			
9a-c	Private investments, jobs and gross value added	This reflects the contribution of the circular economy to the creation of jobs and growth.	Investment Plan for Europe; Structural and Investment Funds; InnovFin; Circular Economy Finance Support Platform; Sustainable Finance Strategy; Green Employment Initiative; New Skills Agenda for Europe; Internal Market policy
10	Patents	Innovative technologies related to the circular economy boost the EU's global competitiveness.	Horizon 2020

**Indicators under development.*
Source: [8].

Table 1.
Indicators on the circular economy included in the monitoring framework.

6. Assessment of circularity of European economic development: first findings

The analyses of data for the ten indicators of the monitoring framework provide a broad picture of increase the circularity of the EU's economy [8]. The areas of the European economic development where circularity is of importance could be characterised as follow:

Production and consumption: progress can be observed toward more circular trends in production and consumption e.g. in terms of waste generation; considerable room for narrowing the gap in performance between Member States and across materials. The EU is largely self-sufficient for most non-metallic minerals such as construction materials and industrial minerals; for the EU's critical raw materials [12] the EU is relying on imports to a large extent, which highlights the need for secure access and diversification of supply[3]. EU municipal waste[4] generation per capita has dropped by 8% between 2006 and 2016 to an average of 480 kg per capita per year; large

[3] E.g. cobalt for batteries used in electric cars, silicon for solar panels.

[4] Waste from households and in public spaces and similar waste from other sources.

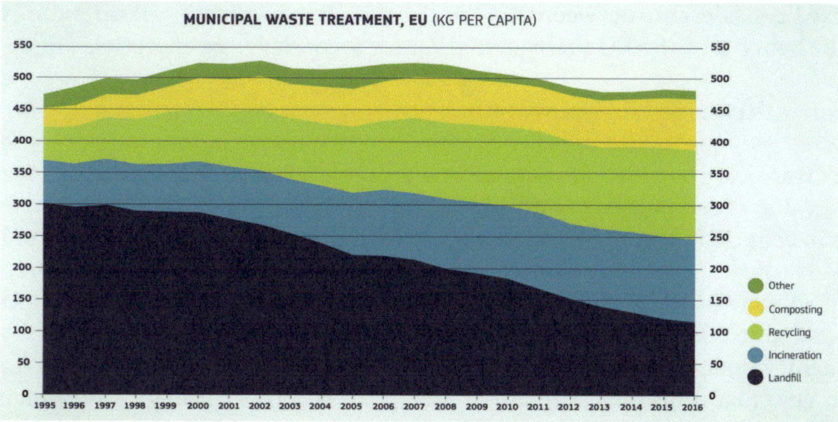

Figure 3.
Municipal waste treatment, EU (kg per capita). Source: Eurostat.

variations among Member States are observed (between 250 and 750 kg per capita per year)[5], and municipal waste generation is still growing in several Member States.

It is positive that the data on total waste generation (including industrial and commercial waste but excluding major mineral waste) per unit of GDP shows a decrease of 11% since 2006. According to Eurostat's preliminary estimates, EU food waste decreased from 81 to 76 million tonnes (i.e. by around 7%) between 2012 and 2014, equivalent to a drop from 161 to 149 kg per capita.

Waste management: between 2008 and 2016, EU recycling rates for municipal waste increased from 37–46% (See: **Figure 3**.). Five Member States recycle more than half of their municipal waste, while some countries are approaching the 2030 recycling target of 65% proposed by the Commission, however, five Member States are still below 25%.[6]

Between 2008 and 2015, the recycling rates for packaging waste also increased in the EU, from 62–66%; it increased in almost all Member States, and in 2015 almost all Member States had met the 2008 target of 55% (the Commission has proposed a target of 65% by 2025 and 75% by 2030 [12]). For plastic packaging, the average recycling rate in the EU is significantly lower, at 40%, even though there have been improvements in recent years. The recycling of municipal bio-waste in the EU was 79 kg per capita in 2016, an increase of 23% compared to 2007.

6.1 Secondary raw materials

In the EU, the level of demand for raw materials exceeds what could be supplied even if all waste were turned into secondary raw materials. Therefore, the supply of primary raw materials will remain necessary. On average, recycled materials only satisfy around 10% of the EU demand for materials, in spite of a steady improvement since 2004. For a number of bulk materials, secondary raw materials satisfy over 30% of total demand for materials (e.g. copper and nickel). The EU is a net exporter of several major recyclable waste streams such as plastics, paper and cardboard, iron and steel, copper, aluminium and nickel. Trade within the EU of plastics, paper and cardboard, copper, aluminium, nickel and precious metals waste

[5] Differences in the way Member States measure waste generation can explain some of the differences.

[6] Member States are using different methods to calculate recycling rates, which can explain part of the differences. The Commission has proposed a common method in its legislative proposal on waste.

increased considerably between 2004 and 2016, allowing economic operators to reap the benefits of the EU internal market for secondary raw materials [13].

6.2 Competitiveness and innovation

The transition to a circular economy is accompanied by an increase of investments, value added and jobs, and stimulates innovation. In 2014, private investments in economic sectors relevant to the circular economy[7] are estimated to have been 0.1% of the GDP. There were more than 3.9 million jobs in these sectors, having an increase of 2.3% compared to 2012. The circular economy sectors created value added in 2014 an increase of 6.1% compared to 2012. Significant role for these achievements play EU funding programmes, available to support the transition to a circular economy, such as the European Fund for Strategic Investments, the European Structural and Investment Funds, Horizon 2020 and the LIFE programme. In in January 2017 a Circular Economy Finance Support Platform was launched.

For patents on recycling and secondary raw materials, the data show an increase of 35% between 2000 and 2013. EU patents for glass recycling represent 44% of the world total for such patents, while the EU's share is 18% for plastics and 23% for paper.

Concluding the analysis of the above figures we could assume the transition to a circular economy is taking place in the European Union. For the period 2012–2014 the circular economy sectors created 3.9 mln. Jobs, contributed to the increase of 6.1% value added in 2014 (Euro 141 billion), compared to 2012, attracting private investment of Euro 15 bln. Circular economy is realised as a vital necessity and has become an important part of the strategy and of policy making of the society. Thus it has become an integral part of the goals of economic development.

7. Conclusions

The chapter provides some arguments for understanding circular economy as a new stage of economic development, where the goal is to meet the challenges of tensions in globalised world, which are strongly connected to resources in limited quantities. The content of the goal is transforming, addressing not only resource productivity and efficiency, but also waste minimization, and many other areas of circularity. The analyses have shown market forces are limited and not strong enough to achieve the new goal of economic development, reflecting the needs of society, vital for its future. It was shown the Hegelian doctrine for economic development provides instruments for understanding and solving new challenges. The new instruments include state regulation and respective monitoring, analysing and drawing conclusions and recommendation, using new indicators, developed for monitoring economic processes and for new economic policies concerning achievement of the new goals of society.

The above notion is argumented on the case of Europe: A new policy for a new stage of economic development focused on circularity on European level has taken place, first achievements are registered. This new policy, in Hegelian tradition, includes A state regulation, aimed at SUSTAYNING economy IN ORDER TO

[7] I.e. reuse and recycling activities. Renting and leasing activities can also contribute to circular economy, but are for now not included because current statistics may not distinguish with sufficient granularity those activities that clearly contribute to circular economy from those that do not. For further details, see the Staff Working Document.

CONTRIBUTE TO ACHIEVING SOCIAL GOALS - preservation of the world's resources, create local jobs and in this way to generate competitive advantages in globalised economy IN ABILITY TO COOPERATE FOR ACHIEVEMENT BETTER COMMON FUTURE.

Author details

Rossitsa Chobanova
Economic Research Institute at the Bulgarian Academy of Sciences, Sofia, Bulgaria

*Address all correspondence to: r_chobanova@iki.bas.bg

References

[1] European Commission. Circular Economy Action Plan. [Internet]. 2015. Available from: http://ec.europa.eu/environment/ci/rcular-economy/index_en.htm [Accessed: 2020-09-20]

[2] Our mission is to accelerate the transition to a circular economy. [Internet]. 2020. Available from: https://www.ellenmacarthurfoundation.org [Accessed: 2020-09-20]

[3] Geisendorf S, Pietrulla F., The circular economy and circular economic concepts-a literature analysis and redefinition. Thunderbird International Business Review 60(3). 2017 .DOI: 10.1002/

[4] Ghisellini P, Cialani C, Ulgiati S., A review on circular economy: The expected transition to a balanced interplay of environmental and economic systems. Journal of Cleaner Production. 2016: 114, 11-3214(7):11-32

[5] Chaturvedi M. Towards the Circular economy. [Internet]. 2018. Available from https://chaturvedimayank.wordpress.com/tag/bio-waste/[Accessed: 2020-09-20]

[6] Mayer A, Haas W, Wiedenhofer F, Krausmann D, Nuss P, Blengin GA., Measuring Progress towards a Circular Economy: A Monitoring Framework for Economy-wide Material Loop Closing in the EU28. Journal of industrial ecology. [Internet]. 2018. https://doi.org/10.1111/jiec.12809[Accessed: 2020-09-20]

[7] George H./ Гегель Г., Избранные сочинения в 14 томах, М.; Л.: Госполитиздат; Соцэкгиз; Л.: Госполитиздат; Соцэкгиз; George Gegel G, (1929-1959) Izbrannie cochineniya v 14 tomah, M.-L.:Gospolitisdat, Sotsekgis

[8] COM/2018/029 final, Communication From The Commission To The European Parliament, The Council, The European Economic And Social Committee And The Committee Of The Regions On A Monitoring Framework For The Circular Economy [Available from: https://eur-lex.europa.eu/legal-content/EN/TXT/?uri=COM%3A2018%3A29%3AFIN [Accessed: 2020-09-20]

[9] The EU Resource Efficiency Scoreboard indicators. Available for 2013, 2014 and 2015. Available from: Eurostat data: available from: https://ec.europa.eu/eurostat/web/environmental-data-centre-on-natural-resources/resource-efficiency-indicators/resource-efficiency-scoreboard [Accessed: 2020-09-20]

[10] Eco-Innovation of products: Case studies and policy lessons from EU Member States for a product policy framework that contributes to a circular economy. [Internet]. 2018. Available from: https://ec.europa.eu/environment/ecoap/sites/ecoap_stayconnected/files/documents/eio_report_2018.pdf. [Accessed: 2020-09-20]

[11] COM/2018/029 Final Communication from the Commission to the European Parliament, The Council, The European Economic and Social Committee and the Committee of the Regions on the 2017 List of Critical Raw Materials for the EU. [Internet]. 2018. Available from: https://eur-lex.europa.eu/legal-content/EN/TXT/?uri=CELEX%3A52017DC0490, [Accessed: 2020-09-20]

[12] COM 595 final. Proposal for a Directive of the European Parliament and of The Council amending Directive 2008/98/EC on waste. [Internet]. 2015. Available from https://eur-lex.europa.eu/resource.

html?uri=cellar:c2b5929d-999e-11e5-b3b7-01aa75ed71a1.0018.02/DOC_1&format=PDF[Accessed: 2020-09-20]

[13] COM (2015) 596 final. Proposal for a Directive of the European Parliament and of The Council Amending Directive 94/62/EC on packaging and packaging waste

Chapter 2

Sustainability Route for Industry 4.0: The Future of Global Circular Economic Transition

Smitha Chandran Sreedevi
and Razim Mohammed Salahudeen

Abstract

The traditional linear models have proved to be ineffective in perspective of the limited resources of the earth and there is an intensifying stress on the resource side due to the ever-rising global population. Moreover, this results in the unsustainable and inefficient consumption of natural resources, increasing costs of commodities and volatility in the markets, which are unaffordable for the manufacturing base of our economy. The current business models based on the traditional economic policies are not only blindly followed globally but they also neglect the organizational specifics. The circular economy or closed-loop economy is an approach in which the waste or residuals from an industry can be used as raw material for another industry there by reducing the demand on earth's natural resources. The expected ultimate goal of this circular system is the reduction of gap between the organizational characteristics like profitability, organizational structure and decision making policies, market position and the adoption of circular economic practices.

Keywords: sustainability, Environment Management Systems, industry 4.0, economic development, circular economy, carrying capacity

1. Introduction

The idea is to dream about an economic model where the products that we use today are tomorrow's resources which results in creation of a cycle that encourages development in this world running by a limited amount of resources. Therefore, it is equally important to address some of the numerous challenges in the present scenario. Traditional linear paradigm (take-make-dispose) has proved to be inefficient in perspective of the finite resources of the earth and there is a mounting stress on the resource side due to the ever-rising global population. In addition, this results in the unsustainable and inefficient consumption of natural resources, increasing costs of commodities and volatility in the markets, which are unaffordable for the manufacturing base of our economy. As an imminent response to these upcoming challenges, we should adopt a circular economic model thereby shifting the current economic model of 'take-make-dispose' to designing products capable of regeneration which should also be accompanied by secondary benefits such as innovations and growth in employability of the economy. The time has come to provide the deserving importance to the circular economy, which is the only plausible and deep-rooted solution to our present challenges and future endeavors.

As we all know, the future is Industry 4.0 which is considered globally as the fourth industrial revolution. The world as we know it is going through its imminent transformation from traditional business models to a digitalized era and it is imperative to us to discuss the impacts and outcomes of this transition towards the ecological and economical sustainability of the world as well as how the circular economic model will be adapting to this massive transformation. Industry 4.0 and the related digitalization of industries are undergoing an exponential progress. While an individual's life is reshaped by the tremendous advancement of industrial digitalization, the world is optimistically looking forward to its impact on Sustainability. According to the MICMAC analysis conducted by reveals that production efficiency and business model innovation which are the economic sustainability functions are the one to be impacted as an immediate outcome of Industry 4.0, which in turn leads its way to the advancement of socio-ecological sustainability functions of Industry 4.0 which are social welfare improvement, reduction of harmful emissions and energy sustainability [1]. This chapter provides a deeper understanding of what the digital industrialization can offer for sustainability and also measures to make sure that I4.0 delivers the expected sustainability functions globally effectively, equally and fairly.

2. Current Economic Paradigm: Linear Economy

Even though the current economic paradigm followed in a global scale underwent radical evolution and development over the years, the economy still sticks to the fundamental characteristic, which came to action during the initial stages of industrialization. The linear economic model which follows the cycle of 'take-make-dispose' has proved to be inefficient and not resource friendly in the long run. Industries source materials, implement labor force to manufacture the desired product and is sold to a customer- 'which in turn he discards after use' does not fulfill the purpose of sustainable development which is really hot topic required at a global scale. However, large-scale improvements are undertaken in the current model, any code, which does not concentrate on economic and restorative consumption of finite resources, will lead to imminent losses throughout the value string [2–5].

In the recent past, many companies started to surface the disadvantages and risks related with the linear economic model. The most notable risks is the surge of resource prices which tangles the businesses between the unchangeable demand expressed by consumer markets on one side and the mercurial and precarious market prices of raw materials on the other. The inconsistent prices are likely to remain on the higher note as the populations rise and urbanize, resource sourcing reaches unreachable destinations and the associated risks to the environment increases. To counter-act this backdrop, a new industrial model was necessary which would answer the questions of efficient utilization of resources and which aligns with sustainable ecological development [6, 7]. The term 'Circular economy' symbolizes a restorative design. It encompasses a cycle of using and reusing of natural sources with maximum possible efficiency throughout the life cycle of finished products and the basic principle behind being:

- Balancing the consumption of finite renewable resources and controlling and preserving finite stocks
- Circulation of the products and its basic materials in value at the best level achievable thereby leading to the optimization of resources.
- Elimination negative externalizations by implementation of effective methods.

With this expected transition, the central role of economic process will be taken over by unlimited resources like labor and the limited natural resources will play a supporting role. Numerous industries were successful in counter-action of the imbalance between supply and demand for natural resources.

3. Limitations of Linear Economy

The present scenario, which is 'take-make-dispose' model, leads to the significant wastage of finite natural resources. Even though throughout our past, the decrease of cost of resources have paved way for economic growth, this low costs of resources related to labor cost has led to the present economic model we follow which encompass wastage of resources on a significant scale. While considering the ease of getting our hands on new raw materials and the cheap cost related to the disposal of the residual, the re-usage of materials has never been our chief economic priority. Various factors affect the capability of self-correction of the system. The present rules, both accounting and managerial has let on for a wide array of secondary costs to be not put into accounts and are considered as externalities. In addition to this, certain products such as pharmaceuticals and fertilizers are to be faced with long approval periods, which is also a drawback to the change [8, 9]. The resulting model known as the linear model works in a non-complex way. Companies' source raw materials manufacture the products and sell them to their respective customers which are then discarded when the products reach their end-of-life. The resource wastes involved in this model are briefed below:

i. Misuse of raw materials during production process: Significant amount of materials are usually lost during the manufacturing processes of products mainly in the sequence amid the initial and final process. For example, SERI (Sustainable Europe Research Institute) came into conclusion that in OECD countries during their manufacturing processes expend about 21 billion tons of materials, which has no direct involvement in products themselves like elements, which has no role in economic system - like segregation of materials from mining, wood and agricultural losses, also materials from construction activities. Wastage of substances takes place in different steps during production. Field damages due to attack of pests and pathogens, production related losses due to lack of efficiency, losses happen because of inappropriate storage condition of goods and products wasted use to inefficient usage by the consumers. The global wastage contributed by the food supply chain adds up to roughly one-third of produced food per year for human consumption.

ii. Wastage by end of life: For majority of the goods, elementary manufacturing rates are greater when compared to traditional restoration rates of goods after the end of their useful life cycle. Based on quality, the global economic system saw a rise of approximately sixty-five million tons of raw materials in 2010 which is expected to rise up to eighty-two billion in 2020. In Europe, approximately only 40% of the total waste materials were recycled of the total 2.7 billion tons of waste. While the sole waste streams are taken into consideration, the present recycling rates cover only a few waste types. The latest UNEP report states approximate losses are calculated only for specific industries of certain level. Rubble created as a result of construction and demolition of buildings contributes to twenty-six percentage of the entire non-industrial solid waste produced by the United States, which consists of countless recyclable materials from wood to steel and concrete. The complete re-usage happens only for 20–30% of all the construction and demolition wastes and this is usually because all structures are built up making them unfriendly to smashing down into recyclable or reusable components, which will ultimately lead to wastage of materials beneficial for the organization.

iii. Utilization of energy: In a linear system, whenever a material is disposed in a junkyard, it indicates the disappearance of all its residual energy. Re-usage saves more energy when compared to the merge share of energy redeemed by recycling disposed products. One of the most intense parts of the supply chain system is the usage of power resources in a linear production model. For instance, the procedures involved in extorting materials from the earth and its transformation to a commercial form favorable to access. During aluminum products manufacturing, the procedures involved in partially finished aluminum explains eighty percentage of energy absorbed. This is because of a system, which depends upon upstream production that leads to energy conservation. Upstream production means no new materials are used every time a product is manufactured and the industry along with its customers are relentless in ensuing immense recycle rates (In Ref. to the stats of UNEP, the 'end of life' rates of recycling of aluminum is between 43–70% and is higher compared to other non-ferrous metals, for example, copper (43–53%), zinc (19–52%), magnesium (39%)). While energy consumption by biological inputs is evenly extended throughout the value chain, the circular mode, which encompasses a reduced energy magnitude, leads to a decrease in the threshold energy demand and helps in the transition towards renewable energy thereby creating a virtuous cycle.

iv. Erosion of ecosystem services: Even though it's as significant as climatic change but given minor s concentration compared as the deterioration of 'ecosystem services' The benefits provided by the ecosystem that bolsters and boost up human well-being, for instance, forests which being a fundamental equivalent of atmospheric, soil and hydrological systems, take in atmospheric CO2 and releases O2, contributes to the carbon content in the soil and also regulates underwater tables --along with further other benefits, are subjected to human mismanagement. The investigation undertaken by the Millennium Ecosystem Assessment on 24 environmental services ranging from immediate services like food arrangement to much more ambitious benefits like pest control and regulation of related diseases found out that 15 out of the twenty-four benefits are corrupted. We are currently consuming beyond the capacity that can be met by the earth's ecosystem, thereby depleting the earth's natural assets. If should be backed up by an example, according to The Economics and Ecosystem and Biodiversity, China lost around 12 billion US dollars in the period between 1950 and 1998 due to deforestation. The economic growth is weighed down due the imbalances of the current economic model:

The troubles present in the current economic system followed which ignores the complete utilization of the potential of natural resources have surfaced as the increase in the commodity prices are becoming evident and also their volatility. From 2002, we have observed a continuous hike in the costs of natural resources. While referring the McKinsey's Commodity Price Index (2011), the mathematical average of the commodity sub-indices mainly metals, energy, food and other non-agricultural products, have reached a higher level when compared to past century values. The most attention worthy commodity price hike was that of West Texas crude oil—147USD per barrel price, which was record breaking in 2008 and in addition, 107% increase in price of food grains from June 2010 to January 2011. The already weakened global economy was further subjected to blow by the sustained higher cost of resources [10–12]. Over the past years, the commodity price volatility was affected by numerous factors. Firstly, the metal prices reached a higher level, much more that their respective cost curves, due to a spike in demands—where it was forced to face the relatively high costs to produce an additional unit. This lead to a condition where a minor change in the demand can result to disproportionately large swings of resource costs. In addition, at the same time, the technological requisites for extracting numerous commodities increased due to the excessive pressure on the easy to access reserves, making malfunctions more common in area of resource accessibility, thereby causing disruptions in the supply chain. The supply dynamics has also been made vulnerable by the weather patterns and abrupt political changes. Finally, the new investors of the financial market was given access to the commodity price tags due to development and innovations in the financial market which in turn paved way to the worsening of price swings. All these factors all-together hindered the global business growth and thus the economic growth. The recent problem faced by the company Tata Steel was that the price of raw materials for the steel manufacturing faced a hike but the steel market did not rise enough to cancel off the higher material cost leading to a loss. The way the companies found out to limit their exposure to this constantly fluctuating cost swings is by hedging contracts at a cost [12–15]. The cost of hedging depends upon the credit rating of a company and the predicted changes in the market. However, in the current economic scenario, the company, which does not possess a grade credit history, will be most likely to spend more than 10% of hedged amount to financial services.

4. Circular Economy

The term Circular Economy has gained popularity in the recent times. The concept puts forth a characteristic and more defined propaganda which is restorative and regenerative by nature while maintaining its primary objective of keeping utilities, products and materials at the highest utility and values at all times. The circular economic model overlooks the presently followed take-make-waste industrial model and strives to redefine social-economical-ecological growth concentrating on positive society-wide benefits. The model progressively decouples the economic activity from over utilizing the finite natural resources and tries to eradicate waste production out of the system [16]. The circular model builds economic, natural and social capital by promoting a transition towards renewable energy resources and CE is based on three basic principles:

- Preservation of natural capital via balanced renewable resource flows and controlled finite stocks: This is carried out by dematerialization of utilities or virtual deliver of utilities. Whenever there is a need for resources, the circular system makes an educational choosing of technologies and processes which uses renewable and better performing resources wherever possible. These approaches enhance natural capital and devise conditions for regeneration.

- Circulating materials and products in the usage cycle while maintaining its highest utility: The proposed circulation is executed by designing products feasible for recycling, refurbishing and remanufacturing thereby providing towards the economy. Tighter inner loops are employed by the circulating system whenever possible which basically means maintenance instead of recycling. This helps in preserving the embedded energy and also maximization of the consecutive cycle counts and time utilized in individual cycles by increasing product lifespan and optimization of reuse. Circular systems also boost the re-entry of bio-nutrients into the atmosphere safely for decomposition which will turn into precious raw materials for a new cycle. In case of the biological cycle, the intention behind product design is to make them consumable or metabolized by the economy and to be regenerated as a new resource value.

- Designing out negative externalities: In CE, waste does not exist as it is designed out purposely. Biological products are returned to the soil by employing biodegradable procedures as they are non-toxic. For technical materials- they are made to be recovered and upgraded there by reducing the inflow of energy and increasing the preserving value of products.

Further, CE believes that diversity important for building strength and it is considered as a major player for adaptability and flexibility. For instance, in living systems, biodiversity is very much needed for surviving environmental changes. Same as that, economies require a balance of businesses to survive and flourish in the long term. While smaller enterprises bring alternate models during crises, larger enterprises put forth volume and efficiency.

5. Value Creation for Circular Economy

- Value of a product is most preserved when it is repaired and maintained to its complete utilization. When it comes to an extend where maintenance is not recommended, then the constituents are reused or remanufactured. The practice preserves greater value against recycling the materials.

- Maximization of the count of successive cycles and/or time utilized in individual cycle for products which means number of times a product is reused or extension of a products life. The prolonged cycles of an individual product saves material, energy and labor needed to create a new one.

- Diversification of reuse practices throughout the value chain. For instance, cotton clothing can be reused and then can be crossed to the furniture industry as a fill-in for upholstery, and further the fiber can be reused in stone wool insulation for construction. This will avoid the input of unused materials into the economy, which in this case before the cotton fibers are safely returned to the biosphere.

6. Economic Impacts

- Economic growth: Economic growth can be achieved by an increase in revenues from upcoming circular practices combined with the reduction in production costs by improved efficient utilization of inputs. These purposed changes in input and output of economic production habits will have an impact on economy-wide supply, demand and prices, etc. through all economic sectors, both direct and indirect, which will add to the overall economic growth.

- Job creation: The effect on employability depends mainly on the increase in expenditure power supplemented by the reduction in prices, which is expected across sectors and also to the intensity of human labor required in high quality recycling practices and high skilled jobs in remanufacturing. Having said that the employment opportunities is not limited to the remanufacturing and growth within large corporations but is rich and diverse. There is an expected creation of jobs across industrial sectors, in small and medium enterprises, by a boost in innovation and entrepreneurship, by local reverse logistics and finally a new service-based economy.

- Innovation: The driving force of innovation is fueled by the dream to replace one-way products with products designed to align with the circular system and which will help in the creation of reverse logistics networks. The benefits attained from a much more innovative economy are energy and labor efficiency, quality improved materials, improved technological developments and increased opportunities to profit for companies.

7. Benefits of Circular Systems on Enterprises

- Increased security and decreased fluctuation of supply: The transition towards a circular system based economy basically means the utilization of less virgin material, usage of more recycled materials encompassing a higher share of labor expenses, decreasing company dealings with fluctuating raw material prices and also increased resilience. CE also decreases the threat posed by natural calamities/political issues on supply chain networks as there is an access for alternate materials provided by decentralized operators.

- Demand creation for business services: More demand for service businesses are created by the implementation of circular economies.

1. Products at the end of their life are reintroduced into the system by collection and reverse logistics companies

2. The utilization of a product to its maximum capacity or longer life cycles are made possible by product remarketers and sales platforms

3. Information and input on components remanufacturing and product refurbishment is offered by the respective specialized service businesses.

The need for specialized skills in order to collect products, disassemble, refurbish, integrate into remanufacturing and finally delivering products to customers, is imperative and this is where specialized service businesses comes to play. The current enterprises doing these processes are mostly subsidiaries of existing manufacturers, and hence there are new opportunities for new business models. Such responsible business models will help companies to attain a unique insight on product usage patterns which will further aid in the development of improved products, advanced services and also improved customer satisfaction [17–23].

8. What is Industry 4.0?

We are in the midst of a powerful transformation in terms of the way we develop products, thanks to the digitalization of the manufacturing sector. This transition is significant in a way that it is termed as 'Industry 4.0' which defines the fourth industrial revolution ever occurred in the area of manufacturing. From the very first industrial revolution which depicted the mechanization of steam power and water, through the introduction of assembly lines and mass production using electricity in the second, the fourth industrial revolution is the continuation of the third revolution of computers and automation with a further enhancement by autonomous systems fueled by machine learning and data analytics. The definition of term 'Industry 4.0' can vary considerably depending on the point of view, but it can be easily referred as the intelligent and permanent linking and networking of machines and machine operated processes. Serious shifts are undergoing in the manufacturing sector which inevitably dismiss the claims that Industry 4.0 is merely a marketing buzzword. The introduction of computers was considered as a disruptive move during Industry 3.0 as it was an entirely new technology then but presently while Industry 4.0 unfolds, computers are interconnected and they can communicate with each other, ultimately capacitating them to make and implement decisions without the need for any human intervention. This revolution is made possible by the combination of technologies like cyber-physical systems; Internet of Things, the Internet of Systems; which will in-turn make smart factory a reality. These supporting machineries will get smarter as they gain access to more and more data, our factories will be more efficient, productive and at the same time, Sustainable. Ultimately, the true power of Industry 4.0 lies in the possibility to gather and analyze information across machines which enables quicker, more flexible and more efficient mechanism to manufacture high quality goods at reduced costs while the expected results being increased productivity, a shift in economics, industrial growth and a modification in the workforce profiles. With the emergence

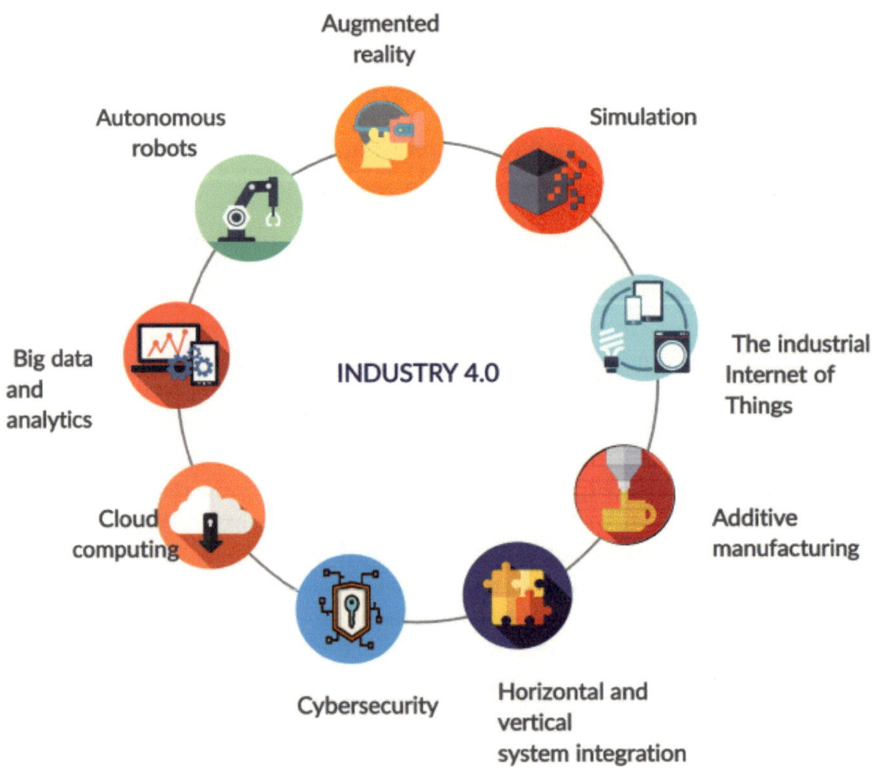

Figure 1.
Components of Industry 4.0.

of new technologies, it is indeed an exciting time for the manufacturing industry as there will be a wave of new opportunities that will help a company towards achieving improved flexibility, sustainability and productivity. The Industry 4.0 will lead this generation towards an ecosystem where humans and machines can work together, empowering businesses to achieve greater insights, reducing risks of error and to make better decisions [24–28].

Industry 4.0 incorporates three technological trends leading the transition which are connectivity, intelligence and flexible automation. I4.0 merges Operational Technology (OT) and Information Technology (IT) for creating a cyber-physical environment (**Figure 1**). This is made feasible due to the development of digital solutions and the advancement in associated technologies which include:

Once dissimilar systems and processes are now integrated across the value and supply chain by interconnected computer systems thus aiding the digital transformation. Embracing this digital transformation with the interdependence that comes along will lead to a multitude of advantages for the company encompassing improved agility, flexibility and operational performance. Even though numerous organizations are operating in denial about the implications of Industry 4.0 on their business or are striving hard to find talent or knowledge to implement the framework, several others are actively preparing towards a future of digitalization accepting that smart machines can improve their business.

9. How to promote Circular systems?

Design and production aligning to CE terms: Primarily, circular economy must be regenerative and restorative by design. Importance must be provided towards the recovery of materials and products at the design level, contrary to the practice of waiting until the end of product life cycle. Design processes should be planned and organized in a manner that will facilitate product reuse, recycle and cross industrial transfer. This intricate CE product design is to be carried out with advanced skills, insights and working plans which are not very popular in the current situation. Material selection is expected to play a critical part in designing resilient products and the manufacturers are expected to detail the purpose of the end products over the specification of materials to be used. Standardized components, design which facilitates ease end of life sorting as well as taking into consideration the usage of by-products and wastes into something useful is also preferred [29–34].

New Business models: New business models should prioritize access over ownership in order to gain more attractive value propositions as this model will transform consumers into users. Companies that can leverage their market share and capabilities in the value chain can drive circularity in the mainstream business. Profitable businesses will inspire other businesses and there is a significant potential to be expanded globally.

Reverse Cycle: For companies to attain value from products at the end of their life cycle, used products must be collected and brought back. Such value preservation will bolster the transition towards a circular economy. This is made possible by reverse logistics and treatment methods which will help those materials to get back on the market. This will be an intricate process which includes delivery chain logistics, sorting, risk management, warehousing, power generation and may even employ molecular biology and polymer chemistry. Reverse logistics network which cascade materials to be used for other purposes is to be optimized totally and must be brought under the terms of circularity. User friendly collection schematics, accessible locations for customers and specialists as well as capability to maintain the quality throughout the diverse applications of the collected products are to be provided significant importance. Efficient reverse cycle will be cost effective, will have a better quality collection and also will employ efficient and effective segmentation of utilized products thereby resulting in the decrement of loss of materials outside the system in turn aiding circular design.

9.1 Advantages of Circular Economy

The world population is growing at alarming rate, so is the usage of natural resources. We will reach to a point where the nature will be depleted of the resources and will not have any to offer the human race. This is when circular economy benefits on a global scale. In addition to using up the resources, the development these days has an adverse effect on the environment. Moving towards a circular economy could offer reduced pressure on the environment. The wastes those are otherwise discarded to the environment are instead recycled and made to use up to its maximum potential. This could improve the security and availability of the natural resources, which are the raw materials for the production processes. This will increase competitiveness among the companies and bring about more innovation, which in turn will boost the economic growth. The economic growth is marked with creating more jobs and other opportunities. Circular economy can also help companies provide more durable and innovative goods with increased quality of life, which help consumers save money in the end [35–37]. According to waste management priority order, the first and foremost priority is to reduce the amount of wastes generated. It is followed by reuse, recycle and other recovery procedures. Disposal of waste to environment is the least desirable waste management procedure. This exactly aligns with the characteristics of a circular economy.

9.2 Circular Economy and Sustainability

It combines the scientific disciplines of management, economy, technology, engineering, environment and society. As circular economy is essential today to promote the goals of sustainable development and all these scientific areas are not independent, their connections and synergies exist and should be further developed. Multidisciplinary approaches and numerous connections between these scientific areas are mandatory to reach the sustainability goals and to solve environmental problems, expand technological limits and overcome potential economic disturbances. This approach is expressed with new policies (market-based instruments, command and control, and circular public procurement), technological suggestions (e.g. technical cycle solutions), environmental engineering technologies (e.g., waste management, 3R strategies, water recycle, wastewater treatment and reuse, renewable energy), circular business models, circular innovations, circular management solutions, consumers' behaviour in circular economy, new circular economy products labels and social acceptance in circular economy.

Journal information.

Nowadays, in the recognized economic systems, goods and services are used, created, and rejected, there is a well-defined pattern in linear economy, where the flow has a clear start and end. The circular economy works relatively differently, the services and products in a circular economy are intended to reused or recycled both in technical or biological cycles. All the products are synthesized in such a way that they can be easily take to bits and the materials used will either be broken down by natural process or returned to fabrication of any other product. The main advantage is that it will reduce the demand on earth's finite resources, also the waste or unwanted residues from industry can be used as resources for another industry. It also provides a well-defined framework that put together approaches and methods from diverse foundations like biomimicry, cradle-to-cradle, ecosystem services, industrial symbiosis, and collective consumption. The circular economy is evidently a diverse way to do business, obliging the establishments to rethink everything starting from resource procurement, design and final manufacture of the products or services. Advocates of the circular economy propose a sustainable world, in which there will not be any depreciation in the standard of life the consumers and can be easily attained without any economic loss of revenue or additional costs for manufacturers and also the quality of the product or services.

Following are the principles that define **how the circular economy should work in the present scenario:**

1. **Any waste is a resource:** All the biodegradable and non-biodegradable materials are use again.
2. **Second hand use**: The product can be reintroduced in the economic circuit after the use by the initial consumers
3. **Reuse**: Some products or certain parts of those products that still work can be reused to elaborate new artifacts.
4. **Repare**: the damage products can be repaired and can be used.
5. **Recycle**: Making value added products from waste materials discarded in waste with or without minor addition or deletion.
6. **Valorization**: hitch energy from waste that cannot be recycled further.
7. **Functionality economy**: it establishes a system of rental property. After the use of the particular product, it is returned to the producer, it is dismantled and the effective parts can be reused.
8. **Relying on energy from renewable sources**: rejection of demand on the finite fossil fuels resources for the manufacture of the product, recycle and reuse.
9. **Eco-design**: This reflects and incorporates in its beginning, the environmental impacts throughout the life cycle of a product i.e. from cradle to grave.
10. **Territorial Industrial and ecology**: instituting of an industrial organizational method in an area/territory branded by an augmented management of resources, flows of resources, stocks, services and wastes.

10. Industry 4.0 as Facilitator for Sustainable Development

The increasing needs and multiplying wants of human beings resulted in the overexploitation of the natural resources. From the primitive cave man to the present computer oriented man, both the volume and methods of natural resources exploitation have undergone tremendous changes. But modern research in science and technology has resulted either in the improved versions of already existing ones or in the inventions of the new ones at the cost of limited natural resources. As a result, the luxuries are becoming comforts and comforts are becoming necessities. Resources are limited, but people's wants are unlimited. Therefore, limited resources need to be used carefully through efficient allocation among the various alternative uses. The rising socio-economic inequality, growing environmental degradation, climate change, urban sprawl and ever increasing cyber-dependency can be underlined as the global tendencies and this may result in social instability, natural catastrophes, water crises, pollution, heavy resource depletion, unemployment and migration throughout the globe [38–43].

After the UN General Assembly in 2015, implemented the Agenda 2030- which amounts seventeen inseparable and self-sustaining goals called Millennium Sustainable Development Goals are envisioned to function as a foundation stone for the renovation of the global economies towards sustainable development. This alteration procedure must result in economic development in agreement with equal opportunity, social uniqueness within the so-called ecological margins. As indispensable investors' for sustainable development, industrial establishments have to move towards an innovative archetype which places much prominence on sustainable value creation. The industrial value creation has undergone thorough changes starting from the age of discovery of fire to the industrial revolution throughout the years. Industry 4.0 (The fourth industrial revolution) which was initiated in 2010s, the ultramodern concept of technology and research for Industry 4.0 and sustainability are highlighted. In response to the Agenda –2030, the European Union released an outline for action, which collectively tells about the planet, people, peace and prosperity [17]. As indispensible stakeholders for sustainable development, all the industrial organizations have to move towards an innovative manufacturing pattern which puts importance on both sustainable development goals together with value creation.The sustainable value creation has three dimensions, such as economic, social and environmental.

The major objectives of industry 4.0 include, linking services, resources and humans in real-time during the making on the basis of CPS (Cyber Physical Systems) and the Internet of Things (IoT). The major physical systems consist of several actuators, sensors, embedded data handling soft wares which enables fast processing and communication of data to different interfaces. There is complete automation in all the systems, process, manufacturing, packing, error maintenance, which helps in easy maintenance and control of the complete system.The value making elements in Industry 4.0 are, Business Models, Value Creation Network and Product Life Cycle, Product, Process, Organization and Equipment.

11. Importance of Sustainable Manufacture in Industry 4.0

The World Commission on Environment and Development (WCED) was appointed in 1983 by the UN to study the relationship between environment and development and it submitted the report in 1987-Our Common Future'. After the publication of 'Our common Future' in 1987, the concept of sustainable development came in to being and is defined as the development which meets the needs of the present generation without compromising the ability of future generations to meet their needs [20]. Sustainable development provides a healthy model for the progress of the world. Sustainable development involves the eco-economic management of resources to reach an optimum level of use and satisfaction, instead of maximum level. It also involves the restoration of degraded resources, maintenance of production and the elaboration of resource base by the wise use of the renewable resources.

As development involves a progressive transformation of the society in all aspects, sustainable development indicates the uninterrupted continuity of the improvement of social, economic. Ethical, scientific, technological, educational and spiritual condition. Thus it is an all-round human development of an integrated or holistic nature. Sustainable development necessitates the rate of depletion of non-renewable resource to be reduced to make future options possible. The national strategies suggested by the WCED for attaining the concept of sustainable development are revitalizing growth, meeting crucial needs for jobs, water, sanitation and energy, guaranteeing sustainable level of population, reorienting technology, conserving and enhancing the resource bases and handling risks and integration of environment and economics in the final decision making [21–24].

Interaction between economic growth and development fully depends on the natural resources and human resources. The attitude of human beings determines both the content of growth in material and energy terms and its impact in terms of equity. Now both developing and developed countries are in the process of evolving sound methodologies to estimate the real stock and the value of national disasters, providing larger and better opportunities for education and health, assessing social and ecological costs of development projects and taking decisions less vulnerability to economic crisis and these resources that are not exploited in enterprises or national accounts. Only if the quantity of decrease in the deterioration of the natural resources and the conditions along with human resources are calculated we will be able to estimate whether growth is quantitatively acceptable or not. Equitable distribution of income, less vulnerability to economic crisis and national disasters, providing larger and better opportunities for education and health, assessing the social and ecological costs of development projects and taking decisions based on it etc. are the different aspects of improving the quality of growth in order to attain sustainable development. Thus sustainable development can accelerate and assure social welfare by taking steps to improve both natural and human resources.

The approach of sustainability comprises of three pillars which include, the economic, environmental and social dimensions as ultimate and integrative arenas of action. Environmental sustainability designates the conservation and existences of the whole ecological complexes, which is both, a source as well as a sink of natural resources and anthropogenic activities. Social sustainability comprises of the equitable sharing of human resources, taking into consideration about the age groups, social classes, gender, and regional distinctiveness together with social justice and solidarity. Economic sustainability needs the keeping of modest benefits and efficient market orientation together with targeting at the conservation of the available resources and thereby increasing the standard of life. Sustainable development involves the eco-economic managing of resources to reach an optimal level of use and satisfaction, instead of maximum level. It also involves the restoration of degraded resources, maintenance of production resources and the enlargement of resource base by the judicious use of the renewable resources.

12. Decision Making with Environmental and Economic Considerations

Economic decisions of the past were taken mainly on the basis of the market value generated as a consequence of implementing the decisions. But quite often markets do not represent the real costs and benefits involved in a particular production process. Therefore reflecting the hidden costs and benefits mainly environmental became a major concern of modern policy makers and planners who aim at sustainable development. Integrating economic and environmental concern proper changes in attitudes and institutional arrangements have become the hall mark of most modern developmental models. Ecological and economic interactions and interdependence and testified through trade, finance, investment and travel. Hence sustainable development requires the association of ecology and economics in order to promote development and safeguard environment.

In the final phase of suggesting essential requirements for attaining sustainable development, the World Commission puts forward the presence of the following systems.

- A political system that fortifies effective citizen's participation in the final decision making.
- An economic system which is able to create technical knowledge on a self-contained and sustainable basis.
- A social system that offers solutions to the pressures arising from discordant development.
- A production system which compliments the responsibility of the presence of the ecological basis for the development.
- A technological system that can explore unremittingly for new clarifications
- An international system that nurtures sustainability patterns of trade and business.
- An administrative system that is very flexible and has the capability of self-correction.

These necessities actually depict the different dimensions of sustainable development. Unless sincere, omniscient, integrated and harmonious changes in attitude take place from the bottom of human hearts, sustainable development will remain a distant dream.

13. Carrying Capacity based Resource Consumption

Carrying capacity is the number of human beings, which can be sustained in a specified area together with the natural resource limits without degrading the social, economic natural and cultural environment for the present and coming generations. The carrying capacity of every system is the maximum amount of resources it can provide and maximum amount of residuals or wastes it can assimilate. Man as an organism has a carrying capacity to use the resources and dump the waste/byproducts back to the environment like any other organism in the universe. If the population of a specific organism is well below the carrying capacity of the environment, it will support positively for natural increase in the number of organisms of the particular species. Several reports are there regarding the carrying capacity of the earth for humans' shows that it has been exceeded far above the normal rate the biosphere can sustain. If carrying capacity of the biosphere is exceeded, living organisms must acclimatize to the new levels of consumption or find alternative resources for meeting their needs. As there is rapid rise in population, the demand for natural resources is increasing in an alarming rate also the pollution load and environmental degradation results. However, through effective management systems and development of new resource saving technologies, we can sustain with limited resources available.

The world Summit, 2002 identified key objectives of sustainable development: protecting natural resources, eradicating poverty and changing unsustainable consumption and production patterns. A multidisciplinary team including technologists, ecologists, economists and policy analysts has to ascertain the consumption pattern globally and determine the human carrying capacity and come up with sustainable solutions in which we are considering both environment and economic development equally. The carrying capacity can be changed by improving the technological advancements. As the system exceeds its natural carrying capacity, leaving the environment no longer able to support even the original number of people inhabiting in the area on a sustainable basis [41–46].

14. Conclusion

For development, we need resources, due to rapid increase in population, urbanization, industrialization the resource depletion is increasing in an alarming rate. We cannot avoid development; we are not able to change to the bullock cart age, so we have to find alternatives for the sustainable use of available resources. We will reach to a point where the nature will be depleted of the resources and will not have any to offer the human race. This is when circular economy benefits on a global scale. In addition to using up the resources, the development these days has an adverse effect on the environment. Moving towards a circular economy could offer reduced pressure on the environment. The wastes those are otherwise discarded to the environment are instead recycled and made to use up to its maximum potential. This could improve the security and availability of the natural resources, which are the raw materials for the production processes. This will increase competitiveness among the companies and bring about more innovation, which in turn will boost the economic growth. The economic growth is marked with creating more jobs and other opportunities. Circular economy can also help companies provide more durable and innovative goods with increased quality of life, which help consumers save money in the end. According to waste management priority order, the first and foremost priority is to reduce the amount of wastes generated. We can follow the reuse, recycle and other recovery procedures. Disposal of waste to environment is the least desirable waste management procedure. This exactly aligns with the characteristics of a circular economy, finally can attain in sustainable future also.

The present work evaluated the prospective of industrial value creation in Industry 4.0 in terms of their involvement to sustainable development. The importance of the study was to put together the social, economic and environmental dimensions of sustainability. The fundamentals concepts of Industry 4.0 and its basic technologies for value development in the context of Industry 4.0, as well as of sustainable value creation were delineated. This work also aims to propose a novel sustainability approach in industrial environment, especially in environment management systems in industries in order to achieve better performance in terms of both economic and environmental perspectives. The work also supports the engineering systems to be sustainable and feasible industrial systems that can support a transition to the circular economy by change in their process, product and approach finally help them to act in fruitful congruence with the recuperative mechanisms of the Mother Nature. Also results in less demand on the earth's natural resources and less impact on environment. The challenge involves complex array of issues and problems that require more sustainable solutions than that are usually done as the end-of pipe-remedies. Hence there is urgent need for environment management together with the incorporation of principles of sustainable development.

Nowadays growing attention has been modeled to enhance the sustainability component in the manufacturing process by decreasing the consumption of natural resources and its key materials, the energy consumption and the ecological footprint which also increases the company's acceptability and competiveness in global markets. The rebuilding comprises of a set of processes or systems, tools and knowledge based approaches to reuse and recover functions and valuable materials from industrial waste products and postconsumer products under a circular economy perspective. Globally the industries are facing several challenges to attain the reasonable and sustainable health by upholding peaceful and good relationship between the societies and the biosphere. To overcome these challenges the components of industry 4.0 is set to achieve sustainable development in three dimensions- economic, ecological and social. The new evolution of the production and industrial process called Industry 4.0, and its related technologies such as the cyber–physical systems, big data analytics and Internet of Things, still have an unidentified potential influence on the environment. Though, the existing economic strategies and the resultant business models are more or less universal, they largely neglect the organizational essentials. The closed-loop economy or circular economy present modewort on debate on sustainable development as it an approach in which the waste or residuals from an industry can be used as raw material for another industry there by reducing the demand on earth's natural resources. The vital aim of the work is to bond the gap between organizational characteristics, such as profitability, market position, structure, decision-making style and the adoption of circular economy practices.

Conflict of interest

The authors certify that there will not exists any conflict of interest in the subject matter or materials discussed in this manuscript.

Author details

Smitha Chandran Sreedevi[1]* and Razim Mohammed Salahudeen[2]

1 Department of Chemistry, Amrita Vishwa Vidyapeetham, Amritapuri Campus, Kollam, Kerala, India

2 Strathclyde Business School, University of Strathclyde Glasgow, Scotland

*Address all correspondence to: smithachandran@am.amrita.edu

References

[1] The Ellen MacArthur Foundation. Towards a Circular Economy - Economic and Business Rationale for an Accelerated Transition. Greener Management International. 2012:97-110

[2] Ellen MacArthur Foundation, McKinsey & Company. Towards the Circular Economy: Accelerating the scale-up across global supply chains. World Econ Forum 2014; 1-64.

[3] Ellen MacArthur Foundation. Towards the Circular Economy: Opportunities for the consumer goods sector. 2013; 12-37.

[4] Yang H. Design for transition to a circular economy. Lect. Notes Comput. Sci. (including Subser. Lect. Notes Artif. Intell. Lect. Notes). Bioinformatics. 2016;**9741**:800-807

[5] Yung R, Siew J. Integrating sustainability into construction project portfolio management. KSCE Journal of Civil Engineering. 2016;**20**(1):101-108. DOI: 10.1007/s12205-015-0520-z

[6] McEvedy, C R Jones, Atlas of World Population History, Penguin, London; 1978.; p. 368.

[7] McKinsey .Global Institute: Resource revolution: Meeting the world's energy, materials, food, and water needs; November; 2011. p. 468-471.

[8] J. Gustavsson C, Cederberg, U Sonesson R. van Otterdijk, A Meybeck. Global food losses and food waste – Extent, causes and prevention. Food And Agriculture Organization Of The United Nations, Rome, 2011.

[9] UNEP International Resource Panel Recycling Rates of Metals – a status report. McKinsey Global Institute: Resource revolution: Meeting the world's energy, materials, food, and water needs; 2011.

[10] Ruth DeFries, Stefano Pagiola. Millennium Ecosystem Assessment, Current State & Trends Assessmen; 2005.

[11] Kamble SS, Gunasekaran A, Gawankar S. Sustainable Industry 4.0 framework: A systematic literature review identifying the current trends and future perspectives. Process Safety and Environmental Protection. 2018;**117**:408-425

[12] 'Oil markets and Arab unrest: The Price of Fear', The Economist. 2011. https://www.economist.com/briefing/2011/03/03/the-price-of-fear.

[13] Climate Change Indicators: Snow and Ice', from: Climate Change Indicators Report, U.S. Environmental Protection Agency; 2010, p. 54. https://www.epa.gov/sites/production/files/2016-08/documents/ci-full-2010.pdf

[14] McKinsey and Company: Transforming the Water Economy – Seven Ways to Ensure Resources for Growth; 2011; https://www.mckinsey.com/~/media/McKinsey/dotcom/client_service/Sustainability/PDFs/McK%20on%20SRP/SRP_09_Water.ashx

[15] United Nations, World Urbanization Prospects – The 2014 Revision 2014; https://population.un.org/wup/Publications/Files/WUP2014-Methodology.pdf

[16] World Economic Forum (WEF), The Global Risks Report 2017: 12th Edition, Gueneva; 2017. http://www3.weforum.org/docs/GRR17_Report_web.pdf

[17] United Nations (UN), Transforming our world: the 2030 Agenda for Sustainable Development; 2015. https://sustainabledevelopment.un.org/post2015/transformingourworld

[18] European Commission (EC), The New European Consensus On Development: Our world, our dignity, our future; 2017. http://www3.weforum.org/docs/GRR17_Report_web.pdf

[19] Bundesministerium für wirtschaftliche Zusammenarbeit und Entwicklung (BMZ), Die Agenda; 2030 für nachhaltige ntwicklung, http://www.bmz.de/de/ministerium/ziele/2030_agenda/index.html, 2016 (accessed 2.12.2016)

[20] G Reinhart (Ed.), Handbuch Industrie 4.0: Geschäftsmodelle, Prozesse, Technik, Carl Hanser Verlag; Ciando, München, München; 2017. https://www.hanser-fachbuch.de/buch/Handbuch+Indust rie+40/9783446446427

[21] World Commission on Environment and Development, Report of the World Commission on Environment and Development; 1987. https://sustainabledevelopment.un.org/content/documents/5987our-common-future.pdf

[22] T Bauernhansl, J Krüger, G Reinhart, G Schuh, WGP-Standpunkt Industrie 4.0, 2016. https://sustainabledevelopment.un.org/content/documents/5987our-common-future.pdf

[23] W R Stahel, The Performance Economy, Palgrave Macmillan; 2006. 269-287.

[24] McDonough W, Braungart M. Toward a Sustaining Architecture for the 21st Century: The Promise of Cradle to Cradle Design. Industry & Environment. 2003. http://www.c2c-centre.com/sites/default/files/McDonough%20-%20Towards%20a%20sustaining%20architecture%20for%20the%2021st%20century-%20the%20promise%20of%20cradle-to-cradle%20design_0.pdf

[25] JBenyus, Biomimicry, HarperCollins; 2003. https://www.harpercollins.com/products/biomimicry-janine-m-benyus?variant=32117835366434

[26] R Lifset and T . Graedel, Industrial Ecology: Goals and Definitions, In R. U. Ayres and L. Ayres (ed.), Handbook for Industrial Ecology, Brookfield: Edward Elgar; 2001.

[27] P.Hawken, A Lovins, and LH Lovins, Natural Capitalism: Creating the Next Industrial Revolution, BackBa; 2008. http://www.environmentandsociety.org/mml/natural-capitalism-creating-next-industrial-revolution

[28] G Pauli, Blue Economy: 10 Years, 100 Innovations, 100 Million Jobs, Paradigm Pubns; 2010. https://www.amazon.in/Blue-Economy-10-Years-Innovations-Million/dp/0912111909

[29] Zhong, R. Y, Xu, Klotz, E, Newman S. T. Intelligent manufacturing in the context of industry 4.0: a review. Engineering, 2017; 3(5), 616-630. DOI: doi:10.1016/J.ENG.2017.05.015

[30] Lanting CJ, Lionetto A. Smart Systems and Cyber Physical Systems paradigms in an IoT and Industry/ie4. 0 context. In: 2nd International Electronic Conference on Sensors and Applications. Multidisciplinary Digital Publishing Institute. 2015. DOI: 10.3390/ECSA-2-S5002

[31] Brook JW, Pagnanelli F. Integrating sustainability into innovation project portfolio management–a strategic perspective. J Eng Tech Manage 2014; 34:46-62. DOI: org/10.1016/j.jengtecman.2013.11.004.

[32] Le, Kao HA, Yang S. Service innovation and smart analytics for industry 4.0 and big data environment, Procedia Cirp, 2014; 16: 3-8. doi:10.1016/j.procir.2014.02.001.

[33] UN General Assembly. Resolution adopted by the General Assembly on 25 September 2015. https://www.un.org/en/development/desa/population/migration/generalassembly/docs/globalcompact/A_RES_70_1_E.pdf

[34] Singh Z. Sustainable development goals: Challenges and opportunities. Indian Journal of Public Health. 2016;**60**(4):247-250. DOI: 10.4103/0019-557X.195862

[35] Ustundag A, Cevikcan E. Industry 4.0: managing the digital transformation. Springer; 2017 https://www.springer.com/gp/book/9783319578699

[36] Batth RS, Nayya, A, Nagpal, A, Internet of Robotic Things: Driving Intelligent Robotics of Future-Concept, Architecture, Applications and Technologies. In 2018 4th International Conference on Computing Sciences (ICCS), 2018; 151-160. IEEE. DOI:10.1109/ICCS.2018.00033

[37] Singh S, Nayyar A, Kumar R, Sharma A. (2019). Fog computing: from architecture to edge computing and big data processing. The Journal of Supercomputing. 2019;**75**(4):2070-2105. https://www.ibm.com/downloads/cas/0WOR6ORJ

[38] Singh P, Gupta, Jyoti K, Nayyar. Research on Auto-Scaling of Web Applications in Cloud: Survey, Trends and Future Directions. Scalable Computing: Practice and Experience, 2019; 20(2): 399-432. DOI: 10. 12694/scpe.v20i2.1537

[39] Tukker A, Charter M, Vezzoli, C, Stø, E, Andersen, M M. (Eds.). 2017. System innovation for sustainability 1: Perspectives on radical changes to sustainable consumption and production. Routledge.

[40] Hammer J, Pivo G. The triple bottom line and sustainable economic development theory and practice. Economic Development Quarterly. 2017;**31**(1):25-36. DOI: 10.1177/0891242416674808

[41] Beckerman, W. 2002. A poverty of reason: Sustainable development and economic growth. The Independent Institute. https://www.amazon.in/Poverty-Reason-Sustainable-Development-Economic/dp/0945999852

[42] Carney, D. 1998. Sustainable livelihoods. Sustainable Livelihoods: What contribution can we make. https://www.environmentandurbanization.org/sustainable-rural-livelihoods-what-contribution-can-we-make

[43] Solanki A, Nayyar A. Green Internet of Things (G-IoT): ICT Technologies, Principles, Applications, Projects, and Challenges. In: Handbook of Research on Big Data and the IoT. IGI Global; 2019. pp. 379-405. DOI: 10.4018/978-1-5225-7432-3.ch021

[44] Das S, Nayyar A. Innovative Ideas to Manage Urban Traffic Congestion in Cognitive Cities. In: In Driving the Development, Management, and Sustainability of Cognitive Cities, 2019;139-162. IGI: Global; 2019. DOI: 10.4018/978-1-5225-8085-0.ch006

[45] Bahrin MAK, Othman M, Azli NN, Talib MF. Industry 4.0: A review on industrial automation and robotic. Jurnal Teknolog. 2016;**201, 78**(6-13): 137-143. DOI: 10. 11113/JT.V78.9285

[46] Nayyar A, Jain R, Mahapatra B, Singh A. Cyber Security Challenges for Smart Cities. In: Driving the Development, Management, and Sustainability of Cognitive Cities. IGI Global; 2019. pp. 27-54. http://link-springer-com-443.webvpn.fjmu.edu.cn/chapter/10.1007%2F978-3-030-14544-6_11

Section 2

Regulation and Control of Economic Development

Chapter 3

Meso Trajectories in the National Innovation System and Their Regulation

Oleg Golichenko

Abstract

The mesotrajectory is presented as a three-phase process of the development of mesopopulations: emergence (origination), diffusion (acceptance, assimilation and adaptation) and retention of a new rule (innovation). The central category of the NIS, i.e. knowledge, is considered from two positions: as a set of specific rules and as the most critical innovation resource. The proposed methodology also describes the three phases of mesostructure dividing each of them into two series–parallel sub-phases and incorporating them in the design of niches, technological and market ones. The methodology allows specifying the effect of the evolutionary selection and intermittent development of meso-units in the first two phases, as well as the mechanisms of changing the socio-technological regime in the third phase. The study set and analyse policy for creating motivation for innovative behaviour at different phases of the mesotrajectory. The actors' mesopopulation are represented as carriers of the properties of knowledge-rules-resources. The knowledge of the actor is taking into account not only as a rule but a factor breaking the mesotrajectory. Among other characteristics of mesotrajectory discontinuity, intermittent equilibrium is taken into consideration in the study. The problem of regulating trajectory continuity is analysed in the framework of public policy.

Keywords: knowledge-rules, trajectory, mesopopulation, factoring populations, incentives and disincentives, technological niche, selection (market) niche, public policy

1. Introduction

The possibilities for applying traditional approaches (including neoclassical theory and theory of growth) and their tools to the analysis of innovation systems are mostly limited [1, 2]. Frequently, the main conceptual statements of these approaches contradict the fundamental properties of the National innovation system (NIS) and its actors' characteristics. For example, it is not always possible to attribute NIS actors to the economic agents, especially in cases when gaining economic benefits is not their objective. Actors are not often represented as agents in the economic mainstream and not always benefit-oriented in short-term and sometimes medium-term perspectives. The actor of the NIS is often considered as decision-making under bounded rationality.

At present, the concept of a national innovation system covers all the major components of the innovation process, including organisational, social, political, and economic factors. Researchers and decision-makers widely use this concept at the regional, national and international levels [3]. At the same time, many authors indicated as one of the main disadvantages of the NIS approach that it lacks bridges between the macro and micro that are inherent in mainstream economic research. According to Edquist [3], when moving to a macro level, the innovation system is regarded as a single entity without breaking out into subprocesses and their actors [3, p. 186]. Here it may just be noted that in the current practice of NIS research, this approach often looks relatively static. Miettinen says that the NIS approach is poorly connected to ... a dynamic way of thinking [4], p. 35.

The neo-evolutionary theory (NET), which has arisen relatively recently [5], is free from these shortcomings). Therefore, to eliminate the shortages and achieve a new quality analysis of innovation development, it seems reasonable to integrate the achievements of this theory and the NIS approach. The following facts indicate that these approaches are compatible.

Like the NIS approach [6–9], knowledge is the central category of the NET. According to [10], the bit of knowledge serves as the nuclear element of evolutionary economics. This bit is considered as a particular rule in the NET [11, 12]. In neo-evolutionary economics as well as in the national innovation system, the emphasis is on the consideration of new knowledge (rules). The NET and NIS actors are knowledge holders; their activity is associated with the generation and use of creative knowledge.

In the NET, the carriers of the same (rather complex) knowledge-rule are combined into a population. It is called a mesopopulation. Therefore, the couple of rule and mesopopulation is taken as a single object called the meso-unit in the NET. The dynamic process of the development of meso-units determines a mesotrajectory [11] or market trajectory [13]. As a result of passing through the trajectory, mesopopulation grows from one holder (entrepreneur or technology supplier) of a new technological knowledge/rule to a population. The mesotrajectory consists of the subsequent phases of the development of a complex rule. They are emergence (origination), diffusion (adaptation and assimilation) and retention of the rule.

It is worth noting that the introduction of the concept of mesotrajectory was an essential step in the development of evolutionary theory. However, neo-evolutionists consider the technological changes that have relatively smooth dynamics. According to the authors, the technological shifts are the result of gradual changes in technologies and socio-technological regimes. Therefore, leap jumping changes in technologies (their mutation) are left out of the consideration of mesotrajectories. At the same time, there are some authors of the so-called quasi-evolutionary point of view [14–17], who insist that radical technological changes are often the result of drastic technological changes that break the previous trajectory of technological development.

These trajectory gaps often result in the discovery of new markets and new industries. The authors mentioned above are also convinced that the emerging technological and market niches, either inside or outside socio-technological regimes, are the drivers of technological changes. The processes of origin and selection of variations in technological changes that can meet the requirements of a changing selection environment take place just there. In the NET, the concept of niches is not actively used and therefore, it is not related to the implementation of mesotrajectories. However, it would be logical to do so. Below we will try to present the process of functioning of niches as a necessary part of the phases of trajectories. To this purpose, we will expand the typology and definition of niches below.

Furthermore, it makes sense to combine the NET and NIS approaches into one concept. The use of mesotrajectory notion in the NIS would make it possible to introduce the dynamics into the analysis of the system and determine the transitions from micro to macro through meso-level. At the same time. The application of the NIS toolkit in the field of public policy in the NET would allow linking the public actions with the need for rule carriers passing the mesophases of trajectories. The embedding NIS in NET allows speaking of knowledge not only as a rule but also as a specific innovative resource. And finally, as the rule-carries' motivation, the analysis of internal and external factors affecting leads to the consideration of new aspects of mesotrajectories usually not taken into account in the NET.

2. External and internal factors hindering the implementation of mesotrajectories and their regulation

Certain factors influence the development of the phases of the mesotrajectories. They can be combined into two groups. The first of them are the factors that are shaped outside of the mesopopulations at the corresponding trajectory phase. The second is formed inside of the mesopopulations of the evolutionary trajectory.

In the first, we include two following categories of risks and uncertainties: 1) inherent in innovation; 2) associated with threats of adverse externalities of technological spillover. They stem from an external environment and determine anti-stimuli for the actors' activities in mesopopulations.

The second group comprises the factors whose elements are formed by some actors of mesopopulations. The actors that fall into a factor forming population are holders of the attributes of a distinguishing factor. Actions of these populations may promote or inhibit the phases of mesotrajectories.

In light of the previous, one of the tasks of public policy is to mitigate the risks and uncertainties. In this study, we do not take into account such external factors of innovation activities as components of framework conditions. The regulation of influence of the factor-forming populations on the trajectory is the second problem of the NIS. The present study attempts to crystallise the mentioned groups of factors and some measures of public policy to regulate their actions. It means that actors cluster the group (populations) of factor characteristic carriers according to the factors.

In this context, it is worthwhile to note that public policy on the evolutionary trajectory differs significantly from the traditional economic, particularly, industrial policy in its goals and role-playing behaviour of the government. Under the general economic (industrial) policy, government actions usually aim at a structural transformation of the economy as a whole [18], economic development and growth of manufacturing and other types of production. Below, the term public or government policy is referred to government regulatory action to facilitate the drivers of a country's development and eliminate barriers [19] or performing core functions of NIS. Moreover, in contrast to the traditional theory, the government has bounded rationality and is only one of the possible participants in the processes of destroying trends of the trajectory and searching and implementing new ones.

And finally, one must take into account that these government's efforts cannot be expected to succeed without solving the problem of encouraging actors to perform NIS functions as well as regulating the activities of factor-forming populations at different NIS levels. This section is devoted to the consideration of these problems.

2.1 External factors for mesotrajectories: risks and uncertainty emerging in the environment

For actors, the activity on the phases of the mesotrajectory has two sides. The first is positive, and it is related to the possible economic benefits of innovation. These benefits generate incentives for the activity of NIS actors. The second is negative, and it is determined by the presence of strong disincentives to perform core NIS function to get these benefits. The high risk and uncertainty of actors' activity lay the groundwork of the disincentives. Consequently, the stimulus must outweigh the anti-stimulus in order this activity takes place.

The disincentives are unevenly distributed along the mesotrajectory. If the proposed innovation is radically new, then the most significant uncertainty of positive results in the innovation activity occurs in the Meso 1 phase. However, if the successful development of the innovation processes provides the transition of the mesotrajectory to the Meso 2, then calibrated risks of getting innovative results will replace the uncertainty.

Risks and uncertainties in the NIS on the trajectory can be conditionally clustered into two groups [20]. The first group includes uncertainties and risks that are natural, i.e. intrinsic and inherent, in actors' activity. Their presence, especially on the early stages of technology creation, does not make firms eager to invest in innovation and support them.

Government, as a partner of an entrepreneur, tries to diminish the natural risks and uncertainties at initial phases of the trajectory. On the other hand, the government's steps may induce NIS actors to act as free riders and encourage them to receive rental income from the corresponding financial help of the government. The government to avoid this phenomenon should strive for such conditions that make actors accept a significant part of the innovative risks and uncertainties. In other words, dualism has to be inherent in government policy.

The dualism means that the domains of public policy will not only compensate for the system of anti-stimulus but also force the participants of the NIS to take on significant shares of uncertainties and risks. One of the methods of actors' compulsion to this sharing is an international competition [21].

The existence of the second group of risks and uncertainties can be associated with threats of adverse externalities or spillover [22] on the mesotrajectory. For example, if an actor was successful at Meso1, he succeeded in such a NIS function of an economic application of new knowledge. Nevertheless, the actor would not receive the full benefit from his innovations without sharing it with competitors, if the spread of innovations, i.e. fulfilment of such a core function as diffusion, took place due to the effect of technological spillover (the unauthorised use of these innovations).

This effect often does not arouse the actors' desire for creating innovations. An actor-innovator to avoid this effect could use substantial isolationist barriers protecting his new innovative knowledge [23, 24]. The durable protection of intellectual property supported by the government can act as such a barrier. However, it must be borne in mind that powerful isolationist barriers may hinder the diffusion of innovations (see Section 3 below). Then such an essential function of the NIS as the dissemination of new technological knowledge can be disrupted. The phenomenon may also sometimes impede the development of the new rules laid down in radical innovations as well as introducing innovative changes in related fields of activity.

In summary, the public policy, the purpose of which is to shape the actors' inducement, should include the following objectives:

1. holding dual policy measures of policy measures, on the one hand, to compensate uncertainties (on Meso 1) and risks (on Meso 2 and Meso 3) and, on the other hand, to force NIS actors to deal with these uncertainties and risks taking on with them through the trajectory;

2. maintaining a balance of performing various NIS functions at different phases of the mesotrajectory.

2.2 Internal factors for mesotrajectories: populations as holders of factor attributes

In addition to the mentioned above factors, uncertainties and risks, the factors formed among the mesopopulations play a significant role in the evolutionary trajectory. They are constructed by some members of the populations in the course of their activities along the mesotrajectory.

Such factors can include:

- Resource capability of NIS actors, i.e. their provision of primary resources (in particular, their shortage or redundancy).

- Firm forms of ownership.

- The technological complexity of innovative products.

- Spatial distribution of innovation processes and actors.

- Technological paradigms in the economy.

- Absorption capacity and its distribution among actors.

As an example, consider a factor such as resource availability or resource provision of enterprises. Let us assume that this level can be low, medium and high. According to these gradations, the set of industrial enterprises is broken down into factor-forming populations of small-, medium- and large-sized enterprises. For instance, these populations can include the following groups:

- Small enterprises up to 299 employees.

- Enterprises with the number of employees from 300 to 499.

- Large enterprises with employees between 500 and 9999, and above 10,000 personals.

The ranges of employees that are available for these enterprises are attributes of such the factor. It worth noting that enterprises within these specified factor-forming populations are not distinguishable; that is, at this level of consideration, the group of enterprises can be considered as homogeneous unless otherwise specified. In this context, for given attributes or gradations of the factor, the analysis deals with homogeneous populations (groups of enterprises).

Now, let us look at another example of factor-forming populations along the evolutionary trajectory. They are related to such a factor as forms of ownership of NIS actors. The sample of actors (e.g. innovative industrial enterprises) can be subdivided into factor-forming populations according to the gradations of ownership the actors are belonging. The structure of gradations can obey a hierarchy. In the case of Russia, it can be presented as follows. At the macro level of the hierarchy, ownership has two attributes, such as Russian and non-Russian property.

Further, Russian property should be split into public and non-public ones. The former has two gradations: federal property and ownership of Russian Federation subjects. The following features can classify the latter as follows: municipal property, the private one, the property of consumer cooperatives, ownership of public and religious organisations, mixed (private and state-owned) property. Finally, last but not the least, the non-Russian property includes foreign and joint possession. The private (52–53% of enterprises) and mixed (14–16% of enterprises) ownership concentrate the main resources (human and material) of innovation. The federal and joint property (19–23% of enterprises and resources) are next in importance.

This just mentioned set of features can be regarded as finite; that is, it is not subject to further division. It means that organisations grouped by the listed attributes are taken as homogeneous regarding the corresponding form of ownership. In this context, it is worthwhile to point out that in other cases, for instance, considering the technological complexity of innovative products, the hierarchy of attributes of the factor must be deeper and homogeneous factor-forming populations of higher hierarchy level have to be split into subpopulations on the next lower level.

Now let us turn our attention to the analysis of dynamics of populations forming attributes such as the resource capacities and forms of ownership in Russia (see also [25]).

2.2.1 The resource capacity

The characteristics of evolutionary trajectory depend substantially on the level of common resources available for enterprises, i.e. sizes of enterprises.

In particular, for innovation-active enterprises of Russia, representatives of populations of small dimension, that is, small and medium-sized enterprises have a significant share of innovative products in their sales. It is worth pointing out that although in 2010–2012 some populations of large enterprises showed growth of this indicator at times, many of them were apparent outsiders (hereinafter, Rosstat data are used). They had had shares of innovative products in sales well below the those of three out of four populations of small and medium-sized businesses. Only the population of enterprises with employment between 1000 and 4999 people managed to exceed the level for small and medium-sized businesses populations.

In 2012–2015, the situation repeated: three out of four resource-rich populations had the lower meaning of the indicator compared to three resource-poor populations. (see **Figures 1** and **2**). However, the shares of innovative products in sales for the enterprises of 500–9999 and 50 to 99 employed became close (16.1% versus 16.2%). It turned out to be significantly below for the class of small businesses employed up to 50 people and the class of medium-sized enterprises with employment in the range of 100–199 people. The values of the indicator for the classes were 17.1% and 18.4%, respectively.

By contrast, it is worth noting that, despite the steady outsider's positions of the large enterprises' populations, they managed to reduce the gap with the leadership positions of small and medium-sized enterprises on Meso 2.

Here, not the last role could be played by the circumstance that the state-owned enterprises belonging to the populations of large enterprises were forced to accept the special innovation development programs (IDP) in which the government drafted the share of innovative products in sales. According to the plans, the enterprises must be answerable to the government for achieving the target value of

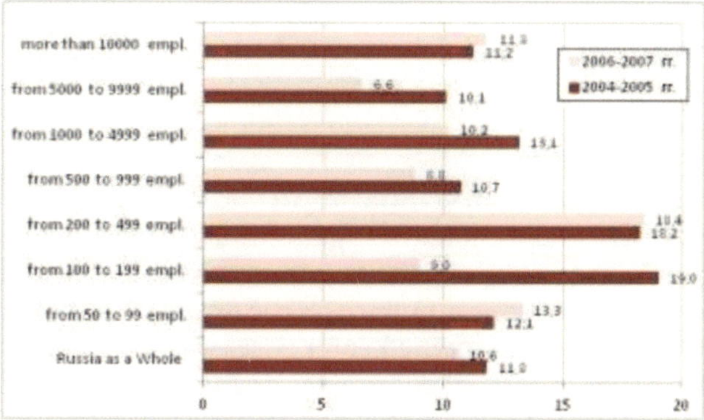

Figure 1.
Average share of innovation production in the sales of innovation-active enterprises by size classes in 2004–2007 (%).

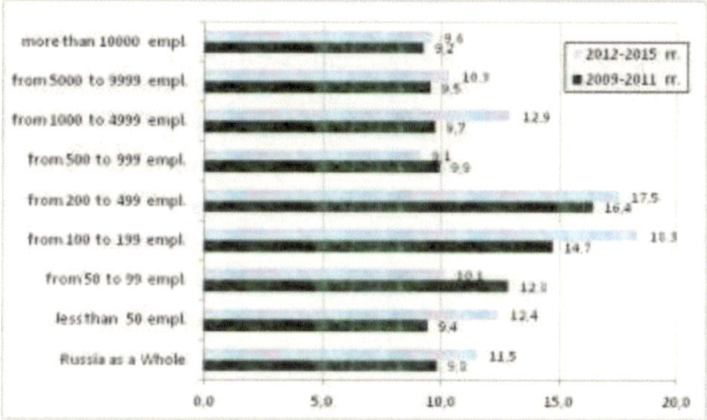

Figure 2.
Average share of innovation production in the sales of innovation-active enterprises by size classes in 2013–2015 (%).

this indicator. This responsibility, posing significant risks of over-statement and falsification of this indicator value for large state-owned enterprises, may trigger the sharp increase of its meaning in these years.

It is worthwhile to point out that in the country the level and dynamics of indicators of the innovation activity scale and economic efficiency along the meso-trajectories continue to be almost wholly established by the populations of large enterprises due to their dominance in the economy. However, as just mentioned, the indicators of large enterprises often point to a lack of their activity along evolution trajectories.

It is essential to overcome the innovative passivity of large enterprises and increase the groups of small and medium innovative business to find a way out of the situation. Furthermore, policy measures are needed to constitute a framework of conditions in the field of entrepreneurship. It concerns, in the first place, reducing regulatory and administrative barriers and developing and providing competitive environments in markets.

The populations of small and medium enterprises had primary positive, innovative attributes. The populations need increasing and supporting by the state. The critical task of public innovation policy is to establish conditions for the rapid growth and prosperity of new firms based on one technology on the mesotrajectories. The urgency of the issue is determined by the fast development of outsourcing processes on the final stages of R&D as well as the traditional disability of large firms to implement quickly new methods of doing business and introducing quite drastic changes in production and delivery methods.

2.2.2 Forms of ownership

The form of property has a substantial impact on the behaviour of the firm and its development and affect the choice of organisational model, management and innovation activity of the firm. The enterprises of private and mixed ownership demonstrate the most significant influence on the overall situation in innovation. In 2015, the number of privately-owned enterprises was 47% (versus 52% in 2006) among innovation active industrial enterprises on Meso 2, along with that the mixed-owned ones consisted 11% (versus 17% in 2006). Consequently, both populations concentrate about 65–70% of the general (human and material) resources of innovation. The next in importance to the influence were the populations of the federal property (15–17% in the number of enterprises and quantities of resources) and joint ownership (7–10%).

For many years, private ownership has not been a leader in entrepreneurial activity in innovation. In particular, the organisations of this form of property has been significantly behind those of federal property. It concerns a share of innovative products in sales (see **Figure 3**). Moreover, according to this indicator, the gap between these forms of ownership has increased dramatically in recent years (see **Figure 4**). Two circumstances can explain that increase. First, as mentioned above, federally owned enterprises had adopted innovative development plans with a commitment to enhancing innovative products in sales dramatically. Secondly, the government had undertaken intensive financial interventions to support state-owned enterprises.

According to the Center for Strategic Research, within the framework of the IDP, there was a significant increase in funding for the state-owned corporations and companies with state participation leading in high-tech industries in 2011–2016. In 2016, the gross expenditures of the state budget on R&D in these companies reached 1.7% of GDP [26]. As a result, the spending on technological innovations of these companies increased more than 20 times (from 2.15 billion rubles in 2010 to 56 billion rubles in 2015). It would seem that this surge in subsidies should drastically enlarge the scale of innovation activity and its effectiveness of these companies. However, that did not happen. The increasing share of innovative products compared with it in the mid-00s was not proportional to the subsidies surge.

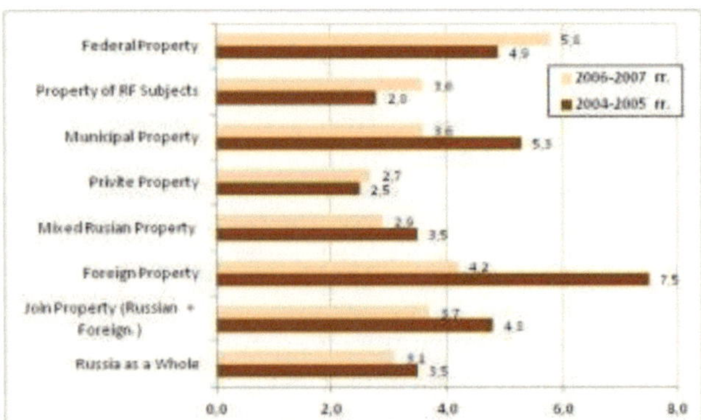

Figure 3.
Average share of costs for technological innovations in the sales of innovation-active enterprises by ownership classes in 2004–2007 (%).

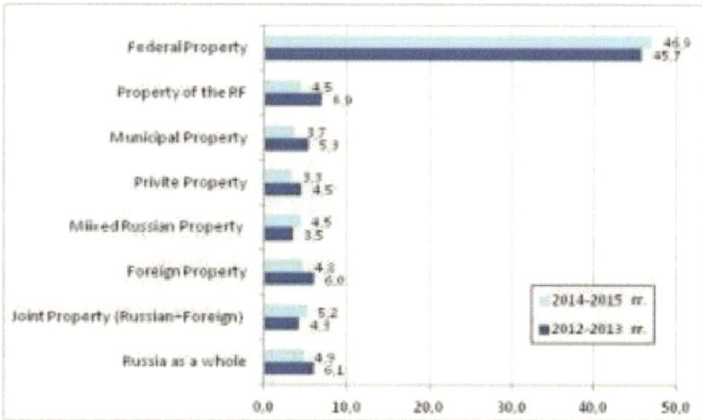

Figure 4.
Average share of costs for technological innovations in the sales of innovation-active enterprises by ownership classes in 2012–2015 (%).

What made the situation even more difficult was the level of innovation efficiency of these state-owned enterprises. It is worth noting that the supremacy of Federal ownership over private property had always been "broken" when one tried measuring the innovation efficiency on Meso 2 calculated as the value of the innovative product per employee. However, this "defect" turned out to be very significant in 2013–2014. If the meaning of this indicator for federal ownership enterprises had been 60–70% of the national average in 2004–2005, it dropped to 12–15% of the average in 2013–2014.

As it follows from the above, the policy measures should be aimed at the following components.

- Forcing the enterprises of private and mixed ownership to innovate, for example, by developing competitive processes in relevant markets.
- Reforming the management of state-owned enterprises.
- Increasing the share of enterprises of foreign and joint ownership in the manufacturing industry, for instance, by creating a favourable investment and business climate.

3. Knowledge as a rule or a resource generating gaps of mesotrajectories

The NIS is often presented as storage of innovative resources and processes that transform these resources [27]. At the same time, the major category of the resources is knowledge, more precisely, innovative rules in the terminology of NET. They play a leading role in providing the functioning of the system.

According to the economic tradition, primary resources or factors of the production process are understood as labour, business, capital, and natural resources. For creating long-term advantages, unique resources stand out among the firm's resources [28]. The resources have a value, and they are rare and poorly replaceable. They have limited mobility, and it is difficult to imitate them [28]. The property of uniqueness of the resources, as it is easy to see, is primarily associated with their scarcity in the economic system. Their supply shortage can be both external and internal. It can occur for ether some entrepreneur population as a whole or for internal subdivisions of a particular focal firm. In respect to a traditional (rivalrous) resource, the internal deficit does not allow the firm to expand outcome and turn into a marginal producer or monopolist displacing less efficient competitors from the market. If the internal deficiency is stable, it leaves no chance for the focal firm to get monopoly rent. Then, the only recourse it has is to receive Riccardo's rent (see also [23, 28]).

However, the situation looks somewhat different when it comes to such an unconventional (non-rival) production resource as the knowledge that provides the birth of a firm's innovation, in particular, a new technological rule. In conjunction with other resources, knowledge has a significant impact on reducing the cost of a product and increasing consumer benefits. The lack of such knowledge among competitors gives the focal firm a competitive advantage in generating and appropriating economic rent. The firm can lose the rent appropriated if particular barriers do not protect the resource from imitation by its rivals. In other words, the firm requires isolationist barriers [22, 29, 30].

It brings up to the question of whether the firm protecting and apply its specific innovative knowledge is always limited to Ricardo's rent. More likely, no than yes. If a firm's specific knowledge is explicit and codified one, such as results of research and development, then there are hardly any natural barriers to its dissemination within the firm. The absence of barriers and internal scarcity suggests that Peteraf's assumption about the dominance of Riccardo's rent does not work in the case. At the same time, it is profitable for the firm to obtain monopoly rent in the market. It has the opportunity if there is an ability to create or use the existing isolationist barriers (in particular, the protection of intellectual property) to safeguard the innovation rule. The barriers make it difficult for competitors to imitating the innovation rule. Consequently, they support the external deficit of the specific knowledge in the external environment of the firm.

From what has just been said, it follows that the use of monopoly rents by NIS actors protected by isolationist barriers results in gaps in a mesotrajectory. The originators of neo-evolutionary theory usually do not focus on this aspect of innovation activity. However, these barriers can significantly limit the processes of diffusion of innovative rules among actors' populations in the second phase of mesotrajectory and even break them. The special public policy measures them reducing are needed to close the gaps and restore the growth of the rule carriers' population.

4. Phases of a mesotrajectory and core functions of the NIS

In the first phase (Meso 1) of the evolutionary trajectory, the emergence of ideas adopted by a mesopopulation and their first actualisation occur at the microlevel. Following Schumpeter's point of view on entrepreneurial activity [31], this phase is dealing with an active entrepreneur showing ingenuity under conditions of uncertainty and risks. Moreover, this entrepreneur is able not only to overcome scepticism proposing a new rule, but he also can take a fresh look at the well-known rule. Besides, he may even find sources of funding for his activities to build a mechanism for the implementation of the new or updated rule. If successful, the targeted actions of the economic agent may change the existing boundaries of entrepreneurial activity and perhaps alter the essence of this activity. At the same time, as current practice shows, a discoverer or carrier of a new rule can be not only the manufacturer of new goods and services but sometimes a consumer revealing demand for products and services not previously produced [32].

In the second phase (Meso 2) of the evolutionary trajectory, the adoption and adaptation of the novelty at the local level, i.e. diffusion of innovation and its support in the economic system, take place. The macro-effect of the phase is the beginning of the destruction of the prior coordination and re-coordination caused by reformatting the behaviour of actors. It is a result of the spread of the new rule. This process of the institutionalisation is an essence of the Schumpeterian approach to economic evolution.

Meso 3 is the boundary and final phase at which the retaining and replicating of the rule and at least the preservation of its carriers occur, and the establishment of a new macro-order takes place. The phase is a well-structured state in which innovation is already introduced into the system, and metastable structures provide the basis of the order. Profit is at a reasonable level; uncertainties have completely transformed into risks; actors' expectations are based on ongoing experiments and comparisons of their results. Technology is widely initialised and adopted by a significant number of users, and markets using the technology are transforming into large-scale ones.

As for the NIS approach, it is worthwhile to note that although here the emphasis is not explicitly made on dynamics, the main (core) functions of NIS processes take after the abovementioned characteristics of the mesotrajectory phases. These functions of NIS can be established from the existing definitions of the national innovation system (see, for example, [6–9]). One can easily see the following ones: creation (generation), storage, distribution (diffusion or transfer) and effective economic use of knowledge. The similarity of the content of NIS functions and phases of mesotrajectories is obvious. However, it is worth point out the task of knowledge retaining is absent among the NIS core functions. Maybe this task needs combining with such a score NIS function as storage. The newly expanded role, on the one hand, ensures the corresponding institutionalisation of the technological regime. Thanks to the task, technological innovation is accepted by a significant number of users and the markets where it is realised become mass. On the other hand, the excessive conservation of the technological regime can generate a track effect slowing down the technological development of the country. Consequently, the mesotrajectory can be presented as a sequential process of performing core functions on the different phases.

Let us also assume that there are two evolutionary mechanisms at work in meso-trajectories. The first of them is the mechanism of natural selection, and the second is the mechanism of spontaneous mutation, that is, the interruption of evolutionary equilibrium. The actions of these mechanisms rely heavily on existing tools for the selection and development of technological and market niches. The niches can both support the functioning of the dominant socio-technological regime and contribute to the formation of a new, more progressive one.

5. Meso-units passing through the phases of a mesotrajectory in the NIS

So, let us turn to the analysis of the mesophases of the innovative development trajectories and split every phase into two sub-phases. We represent Meso 1 as the sequential-parallel processes of creation and diffusion of open codified knowledge (subphase 1.1) and the methods of transforming open knowledge into pre-competitive one (subphase 1.2). Meso 2 contains the processes of shaping a new selecting (market) environment (subphase 2.1) and the development of the pull of this environment (subphase 2.2). Finally, Meso 3 combines two processes:

- formation of an exit from the previous development track (subphase 3.1);
- introduction of a new one, in particular, construction of new mass-consumption environment (for instance, the market for goods and services produced according to the new rule) and maintenance of its metastability (subphase 3.2).

It is worth to note that the first attempt introduces such phase portioning belongs to [11]. However, the proposed partition is somewhat different from that of the just mentioned work. We will not specifically analyse the difference between the formulations. Let us only note that the partitioning does not contradict the meaning Doppfer' one. The terms defining it are closer to specialists whose activities are directly related to the analysis of innovation processes. Besides, we included in the third mesophase the process of destruction of the previous development track, which Dopfer did not single out at the beginning of the phase.

5.1 Mesophase 1: origination of an idea/rule and meso-units shaping

The first phase starts a process of de-coordinating the selective environment (particularly, market) and creating new complex knowledge. In the first subphase, public policy has the objectives: 1) direct support of basic research; 2) creation and support of open information channels, that is, mechanisms for decoding and transfer available codified knowledge [20].

The transmission or transfer of codified information through an open information channel is an essential element of knowledge diffusion. It allows ensuring the process of pre-competitive cognition and technology invention if the acquisition of knowledge that is not special but generic enables its application in a reasonably wide range of areas. It is all the more relevant as the actor is unable to realise an available technological stock without additional scientific knowledge of an academic nature. The absence or ineffective operation of the open information channel creates gaps between the first and second subphases and significantly reduce the efficacy of the latter.

In the second subphase, the government supports for the channel for converting and transforming open knowledge into pre-competitive one [20]. Its content is to keep:

1. the functioning of technological niches implemented, for example, in business incubators or initial stage venture business;

2. intra-company R&D incorporated in setting up technologically new processes and products;

3. NIS actors' cooperation in the generation of pre-competitive knowledge. At this phase, the activity of population actors occurs under conditions of significant uncertainty (see Section 2). The active innovators need information, organisational and financial assistance from the government.

It is worth noting that at this phase, the activity of population actors occurs under conditions of significant uncertainty of a result (see Section 2.1). The active innovators need information, organisational and financial assistance from the government.

Technological niches. Using a niche enables NIS actors to counter emerging threats in development trends (for example, environmental degradation and reducing market demand). In these cases, innovators work in niches in the hope that they will help smooth and diminish these threats, while also through a series of technical improvements will be able to take into account the nature and future dynamics of the pressure of the selection environment.

As mentioned earlier, forming technological niches, it is necessary to take into account that in the socio-economic environment, in contrast to the biological one, there should be a co-evolution of technology and the selective settings [33].

It means that the selective environment is not steady and not exogenous to the evolution of the group of carriers of the technological rules. Therefore, consumers cannot be considered in isolation from producers and investors.

Niches make a protected technological space in which inventions are tested and become a starting point for radically new technologies and products. The actors' population in the niche can include both actors of the previous technological regime and new players, carriers of new technologies. The process of growing technology and evolutionary learning help generate demand for technology and its products. They also include proto-markets, where the first interactions between producers and users of these technologies and products take place. If the proto-market is successful, the technological niche turns into a rather broad market.

The protection of technological niches and their entry into the selective (market) space are organised by NIS actors investing in promising fledgeling technologies. Financial resources for the development of technological niches are private investments in strategic R&D and public grants or subsidies from the target users, for example, defence agencies.

Business incubators, technology parks, advanced technology programs, and support for pre-competitive cooperation between business and public organisations in the development of radical technologies can serve as a form to arrange public support for technological niches. There is a need in policy aimed at actors seeking the status of innovators who are able to create specialised technological niches themselves, and thus resist the established rut of development.

The implementation of the concept of technological niches in many ways enables us to create prerequisites for solving the problem of advanced innovative development, in particular, by forming quasi-evolutionary mutations.

5.2 Mesophase 2: rule adoption and diffusion in the selection environment

At the beginning of the phase, the first adoption of the rule by the market (selection environment) occurs. The randomness of the environment and its bifurcations give rise to uncertainty of innovation rule perspectives. If it is possible to reduce this uncertainty, then the turnover of innovations becomes large-scale [12], the rule belongs to a group. At the end of the phase, the significant population of rule-carriers is emerging. Its shaping allows saying that a mesolevel bringing future innovative changes has appeared in the economy.

Selection (or market) niches created for the new technological rules are tools that give an opportunity reducing the chaos of the environment introduce order and, ultimately, achieving the spread of the new rules among consumers. If the market acts as a selective medium, then at this phase, there is a transformation of pre-competitive into competitive knowledge.

The phase can be represented as two subphases.

At the first of them (subphase 2.1), a new selection (market) environment is shaped. It has a perceptual ability to adopt the proposed new technological ideas. Public policy supports the formation and development of selection niches for them (for example, within the technology parks and advanced technology programs, late stages of venture capital business supported by specialised tax breaks). Besides, to protect emerging niches, isolationist barriers that partially and sometimes completely block the diffusion of the innovation rule to competitors are raised.

At the second subphase (subphase 2.2), a new selection environment develops. It means that there are growth and blurring of the most successful (selection) market niches, that is, a conquest for market space by niche actors. The government innovation policy in NIS is aimed at supporting and developing the demand for new products produced according to new technological rules, new technological knowledge diffusion among producers and consumers. The policy facilitates the reduction of isolationist barriers and provides the operating of channels of commercial knowledge transfer [20] from the niches.

The sub-phases can be linked in the mesotrajectory. As a result, the second one turns out to be a continuation of the first. At the same time, it is worth recalling that the requirements for public policy at different sub-phases may come into an inevitable conflict with each other (see also Section 3). At the first one, the public policy should support isolationist barriers protecting the innovative rule owners. At the second subphase, it may turn out that the introduced protective barriers, being demotivators for actors to enter the population of rule carriers, prevent the expansion of mature niches into the market or other selection space. Therefore, there appears a need for mechanisms reducing the barriers.

This phase has to make certain the progress of the rules at the level of micro and macro inventions that appears in the previous phase, i.e. particularly, implement them to produce products useful to the consumer. A safe space for the adaptation of the rules can be organised in isolated niches (a separate environment). At the start of the phase, a niche product is scarce. However, if it successfully diffuses among consumers outside the niche, it can ensure the steady growth of its market. Consequently, the successful niche might put the corresponding meso-unit on the trajectory of increasing economies of scale.

Types of selection (market) niches. Within the niche, the direction of the evolutionary technological process is mainly determined not by variations of existing generations of technologies, but by changes in the selective environment. However, the changes in the selection environment of a niche can force niche actors not only to reject unsuitable technologies but also create a preferred technology option by organising a step-by-step process of improving existing options. This process of changing technological rules takes place in the interaction of producers and users.

The types of emerging niches should be distinguished both by the method of formation and by their content. According to the first item, we should distinguish two types of niches. One of them includes the niches that are the result of the transformation of the technological niches that arose in the previous phase of a mesotrajectory. The second one singles out the niches that are purposefully created for the organization of local adaptation and evolution of mainstream technologies that maybe are not widely spread in the country. In terms of content, it is necessary to take into account that some niches implement natural selection; that is, they prolong a continuous evolutionary process. In contrast, other niches provide a change in the direction of evolution, that is, intermittent development.

In other words, technological niches are often at the origin of selection (market) niches. As mentioned above, a successful technology niche generates some primary markets build by coalitions of actors-agents to test and develop new technologies. The proto-market can eventually transform into a niche market. The likelihood of such a transformation is high if the technologies presented on the proto-markets take into account a perspective for the co-evolution of producers and consumers in a certain market segment. These transformation mechanisms usually operate in developed countries at the stage of development based on innovations. In the initial stages of this transformation, small and medium-sized enterprises often act as original technology carriers [34].

Following the above, another option for the emergence of market niches is also available. In this variant, micro or macro inventions continuing the trends of the mainstream evolve in market niches. As a result of this isolation, the technology development can lead to the development of the technology for the local environment (including step-by-step improvement of known, in particular, imported technologies or the development and adaptation of inclusive options for advanced technologies). The emerging technology can also diffuse into other market niches contributing to the origination of new socio-technological regime in the economic system. If a certain degree of local maturity of the regime is reached, it penetrates the mainstream markets and begins to compete with the other regime modes that are widespread there. Niches of this development model can be shaped within special economic zones to create a pool of new technologies for the country. The implementation of the pool could be necessary to reduce the gap with the mainstream of technological development. The formation of market niches of this kind is typical for actors in developing countries undergoing the investment stage of development [34]. Moreover, large national companies act as actors of mainstream technology carriers if government organises their protection and support in the niches.

Transformation of technological niches into selection (market) ones. Considering the processes of formation of selection (market) niches for which technological ones serve as a prototype, it is worth to take into account the following circumstance. The radical technological changes are the result of a process of ether gradual changes, accumulated step-by-step cumulative innovation or rapid progressive changes accompanied by opening up new markets and creating new industries [33].

Following what has just been said, one can distinguish niches of natural selection and discontinuous equilibrium.

Niches of natural selection (quasi-classical evolution). In a selection (market) niche, the direction of the evolutionary process is determined not by the variations of emerging technology generations but by alterations in a selective environment. The alterations made actors not only reject unsuitable technologies but also forces them to organise a step-by-step process of improving the existing advantageous technologies. This process occurs in the interaction between a producer and user (see, for example, [32]) Besides, the carriers of the technology should take into consideration not only the market but also institutional factors of selection. As a result of the process, among the actors, the number of carriers of improved technology technologies increases. In contrast, the number of actors who have technologies with features unfavourable for the altered environment decreases.

Niches of intermittent equilibrium. However, periods of gradual accumulation of new technological features characterised by the absence of visible changes or minor shifts can be disrupted if technologies that have an intermittent nature arise. Then there are technological changes that are considered analogous to the so-called intermittent equilibrium, studied in biology [33].

Within the framework of this equilibrium, long periods of relatively steady dynamics of mesotrajectories, which are characterised by the accumulation of smooth evolutionary variations of technological species, suddenly end and there are leapfrogs to new types of technologies. The leaps originate at the Meso-1 phase in technological niches of interrupted (or punctuated) equilibrium. Mutations destroy the selection environment. Therefore, the task of the mesopopulation is to transform the technological niche of intermittent equilibrium into a selection (market) one to begin shaping a full-fledged environment. In other words, the goal is to turn the niche, eventually, into the widespread domain (mass market) that can provide the basis for changing the dominant socio-technological regime.

5.3 Mesophase 3: changing the old rule and retaining the new rule

At the Meso 3 phase, the main role is played by the dominant institutional or socio-technological regimes [35], which establish the prevailing system of meso-unit coordination. The socio-technological regime is characterised by the rules that define the technological (technical) structure and market development (user's preferences), as well as the processes of their regulation. In this sense, a regime is a set of sequential rules that are carried by a certain range of actors including firms, users and government. Changing the system of rules leads to a transition to a new type of mesotrajectory.

A particular socio-technological regime supports the dominant technology genes (see [33], pp. 607). A genotype of technology refers to the rules for how to produce, use and regulate specific products. The technology is considered as the constructions (analogous to the biological genotype) whose implementation in products and processes (technology phenotypes) is promoted by various firms. The functions of the regime also include such actions as transferring and storing the rules (see [33], p. 608–609). The technology genes determine the generality and differences between technological species.

Such components of the knowledge system stipulate the metastability of Meso 3 as routines, competencies, and the ability to use them. Conserving and preserving knowledge (rules) and reproducing them allows actors to create a space for step-by-step technological mutations. In this space, there is a dynamic balance of developing technological types supported by their incremental improvement and improvement.

In theory, a regime exists as long as its rules remain essential for the economic system. The fundamental nature of the rules is to maintain an optimal balance between increasing returns to scale (short-term effect) and the desired degree of diversity, i.e. the possibility of considerable recombination of innovations (long-term benefit) for the existing genotype of technologies. However, this balance cannot remain optimal for a long time due to the internal conflict between the achieved level of economies of scale and the demand for expanding the diversity of technological genotypes. The conflict causes a change in technological genotype after a while. Finding and implementing a new optimal balance may not be easy. Therefore, at this stage, there is a danger to fall into the trap of a well-worn track. In result, a systemic failure of the national innovation system takes place. This trap gives rise to the severe dysfunction of the NIS, that is, the failure to perform such its primary function as gaining and implementing innovative knowledge.

Resistance to changes in ideas, institutions, technologies, and the behaviour of actors can be an additional factor in maintaining the existing track. In addition, one can also attribute some historical restrictions to the resistance factor. In biology, such circumstances are referred to as a development constraint [36] or phylogenetic inertia [37]. In economics, this phenomenon is interpreted in terms such as dependence on the path of development, blocking the future path [38].

However, if a rule carriers' population passed Meso 2 manages to overcome this resistance and shape promising market niches external to the existing socio-economic regime, then the stability of the previous development track is violated. The search for a new technological balance starts, new technological genes that are not a continuation of the existing ones begin to dominate. New evolutionary shifts on meso-trajectories change the order at the macro level, and a new socio-technological regime appears. This mode initiates a new ordered (metastable) state with its structure and order.

Influence of niche development on the change of socio-technological regime. A significant factor in extending a life span or changing the dominant socio-economic regime is the process of spreading market niches. The set of market niches that coexist with the mode facilitates the stability of its functionality. Elements of such niches can be associated with global socio-technological regimes. The existence of the set of niches compatible with the socio-technological regime points out a mosaic of technological evolution. A similar idea of mosaic evolution of branching species is also present in biology [39].

If in the process of their development, all niches remain internal to the regime, then they support various elements of its functionality and realize its internal diversity. In the process of diffusion of innovative rules, thanks to the incremental changes in technologies and rivalry between them, the new socio-technological regime adjusting to the new requirements of the selective environment evolves. Its evolution gives rise to a new equilibrium of the system. In the process of diffusion of innovative rules, thanks to the incremental changes in technologies and rivalry between them, the new socio-technological regime adjusting to the new requirements of the selective environment evolves. Its evolution gives rise to a new equilibrium of the system.

The increased variability of the niches leads to their transition to the category of external ones if the changes introduced in niches are fundamental. The active progress of external niches can ultimately lead to the transformation of the socio-technological regime, that is, the formation of a new evolution direction. In this case, the situation changes radically. First of all, it may be associated with the emergence of market niches of punctuated equilibrium and powerful incentives for the actors of the innovation system to invest in these niches.

There may also be another case when the rules changing so after some correction allow actors of mesopopulation to keep previous dimensions of development. As a result, the dominating regime improves and adapts to the new requirements of the selection environment. For example, the pressure of growing demand for electric cars forces traditional car manufacturers to focus their efforts on meeting environmental needs of the social environment within the framework of the previous model of a vehicle with an internal combustion engine. Thus, the existing socio-technological regime is being adjusted.

As it follows from the above Meso 3 should be divided into two subphases:

1. Getting out of the rut of previous development.

2. Forming a new track of development.

To pass these subphases, it is necessary:

1. To initiate the narrowing of the differences between the country's technology pool and the existing variety of technological genotypes in the world.

2. To determine the dimensions of necessary technological shifts from the positions of existing technological genotypes in the world.

3. To facilitate the penetration of technology genotypes created at the Meso 2 phase to mass markets.

The solution of the first and second tasks determines the conditions for getting out of the previous development track isolated from the technology mainstream. The country must participate in international value chains and use international competition as a driver of the necessary shifts. The result might be the design of socio-technological regime that, on the one hand, has common technological genotypes with regimes of advanced countries, and, on the other hand, satisfy the particular needs of the country's technological development. Carefully thought-out government policy is needed to implement such a manoeuvre [21].

Public policy should encourage the diffusion and development of the wide range of technologies to expand the diversity of those that promote structural shifts towards more advanced technological genes. It can also foster the development of modular technologies facilitating innovative combinations and exchanging information, so that cross-fertilisation or pollination in modular innovations become possible. The use of recombination of technological innovations can be a key element to get out of the rut trap, for example, through switching to environmentally friendly technologies.

6. Conclusions

Thus, one can present a mesotrajectory as a sequential process of performing core NIS functions on the different its phases.

The study of the problems of regulating the mesotrajectory should take into account that the focus must be on the impact of policies on two groups of factors. The first is external factors whose action is manifested in the existence of high risks and uncertainties distributed over different stages of the mesotrajectory. The high risks and uncertainties generate strong disincentives to perform core NIS function. The second group occurs within the mesopopulations, some of whose actors shape the factors of the group and can be teemed into factor-forming populations.

Regarding the first group of factors, two conclusions can be drawn. First, government policy that aims to mitigate inherent risks and uncertainties must be dual. It means that, on the one hand, the innovation system should facilitate compensation for a part of uncertainties and risks inherent in innovation activity, and, on the other hand, make the actors carry a significant portion of risks themselves. Secondly, if the NIS is intended for regulating the effects of externalities (e.g. technological spillover) on different phases of the trajectory, then its task is to reduce risks of their adverse influences on the evolutionary trajectories. In this case, the policy should maintain some balance of these influences on different NIS core functions on mesotrajectories. Notably, it could provide a choice between a strong or weak public support of intellectual property rights.

The actions of factor-forming populations also contribute to realising the core NIS functions on the different phases of trajectory. It is worthwhile to organise support and expansion of those factoring-forming populations that have a positive effect on the phases of mesotrajectories. If the factor-forming population harms the trajectory phases, then the targeted policy should neutralise it, in particular, weakening this actors' population. In the case, when a factor-forming population demonstrates both positive and negative influences on the trajectory, the policy should facilitate a transformation of the actors' behavioural models dominated in the population. It means that it may assist in strengthening the useful parameters of the models and eliminating or smoothing their harmful ones.

A significant limitation of the neo-evolutionary approach is not taking into account the fact that in addition to changing the size of the mesopopulation and transforming the innovation rule, it is necessary to consider also other its characteristics. Among them, innovative resources of the population, elements of the production processes embodying the rule into products and technologies. One of the most critical innovative resources is the knowledge that underlies the technological rule.

Therefore, it is necessary to consider populations of system actors not so much as a set of carriers of the knowledge-rule pair, but as a set of carriers of the knowledge-rule-resource triple. At the same time, it should be taken into account that knowledge as a resource can be a source of innovative rent for actors. The contest for its possession can break the continuation of mesotrajectory. The isolationist barriers built by the firm and the state to preserve the innovative rent rights largely facilitate the emerging gap. This gap gives rise the problem of public regulation of innovation diffusion in mesotrajectories. The problem is not simple. On the one hand, monopoly isolationist barriers protecting market niches promote the development of radical technologies. However, on the other hand, they make a hindrance to diffuse innovations into the market space.

However, the reasons for the discontinuity of the trajectory may not only the factors mentioned above. They can include both the origin and spread of disruptive technologies. The emergence and development of these technologies can disrupt the relative stability and continuity of the former mesotrajectory due to the appearance of significant mutations of technological species. The appearance of such gaps poses difficult tasks of regulating the mesotrajectory and managing technological and market niches.

Also, embedding the design of niches into the three-phase model of mesotrajectories of the new evolution theory is, in our opinion, an essential theoretical and practical aspect of its development. The introduction of a system of niches gives an opportunity to tie together better all three mesophases. Moreover, it allows considering more adequately control loop of the trajectory. In particular, it concerns the incorporation of evolutionary and intermittent development into the dynamics of meso-units at the first two mesophases and the mechanisms for changing or prolonging the span of the socio-technological regime at the third phase.

Author details

Oleg Golichenko
Central Economics and Mathematics Institute of Russian Academy of Sciences, Moscow, Russia

*Address all correspondence to: golichenko@rambler.ru

References

[1] Lundvall B-A, Johnson B. The learning economy. Journal of Industry Studies. 1994; 2: pp. 23-42.

[2] Golichenko O. The national innovation system: From concept to research methodology. Problems of Economic Transition. 2016; 58: 463-481.

[3] Edquist C. Systems of Innovation: Perspectives and Challenges. In Nelson RR, Mowery DC, Fagerberg J editors. The Oxford Handbook of Innovation. Oxford: Oxford University Press; 2006. p. 181-208.

[4] Miettinen R. Innovation, Human Capabilities, and Democracy: Towards an Enabling Welfare State. Oxford: Oxford University Press; 2013.

[5] Dopfer K, Potts J (editors). The New Evolutionary Economics. Edward Elgar Publishing; 2014.

[6] Freeman. C. Technology Policy and Economic Performance: Lessons from Japan. London and New York: Pinter Publishers; 1987.

[7] Lundvall B Å (editor). National Systems of Innovation. Towards a Theory of Innovation and Interactive Learning. London: Pinter; 1992.

[8] Nelson RR. National Innovation Systems: A Comparative Analysis. New York: Oxford University Press; 1993.

[9] Metcalfe S. The economic foundations of technology policy: equilibrium and evolutionary perspectives. In: Stoneman P, editor. Handbook of the Economics of Innovation and Technological Change. Blackwell Publishers. Oxford (UK)/ Cambridge (US); 1995.

[10] Dopfer K, Potts J, Pyka A. Upward and Downward Complementarity: The Meso Core of Evolutionary Growth Theory. Springer-Verlag Berlin Heidelberg; 2015.

[11] Dopfer K. Foster J, Potts J. Micro-meso-macro. Journal of Evolutionary Economics. 2004; 14: 263-279

[12] Dopfer K. The origins of meso economics. Schumpeter's legacy and beyond. Journal of Evolutionary Economics. 2012; 22: 133-160.

[13] Bleda M, del Rio P. The market failure and the systemic failure rationales in technological innovation systems. Research Policy. 2013; 42: 1039-1052.

[14] Schot J W. The policy relevance of the quasi-evolutionary model: The case of stimulating clean technologies. In: Coombs R et al, editors. Technological Change and Company Strategies. London: Academic; 1992: 185-200.

[15] Kemp R, Schot J, Hoogma R. Regime shifts to sustainability through processes of niche formation: the approach of strategic niche management. Technology Analysis and Strategic Management. 1998; 10: 175-196

[16] Hoogma R, Kemp R, Schot J, Truffer B. Experimenting for Sustainable Transport: The Approach of Strategic Niche Management. London: Spon. Press; 2002.

[17] Raven RPJM. Strategic Niche Management for Biomass. The Netherlands: Eindhoven University; 2005.

[18] Bianchi P, Labory S. From 'old' industrial policy to 'new' industrial development policies. In: Bianchi B, Labory S, editors. International Handbook on Industrial Policy. Cheltenham: Edward Elgar; 2006: 3-27.

[19] OECD. Governance of Innovation System. Paris: OECD; 2005.

[20] Golichenko O. The Methodology of national innovation system analysis. In: Latif Al-Hakim, Chen Jin, editors. Quality Innovation: Knowledge, Theory, and Practice. USA: Hershey Pennsilvanya, 2013: 94-123.

[21] Golichenko O. Public policy and the failures of the national innovation system. (In Russian). Voprosi Economici. 2017; 2: 1-12.

[22] Golichenko O, Samovoleva S. The balance of externalities and internal effects in national innovation systems. In: Proceedings of the 10th European Conference on Innovation and Entrepreneurship; 17-18 September 2015; Genoa, Italy; 2015. p. 223-230

[23] Peteraf M. The cornerstones of competitive advantage: a resource-based view. Strategic Management Journal. 1993: 14: 179-191.

[24] Peteraf M, Barney J. Unraveling the resource-based tangle. Managerial and Decision Economics. 2003; 24; 309-323.

[25] Golichenko O. Regulation of meso trajectories in the national innovation system. In: Proceedings of the 14th European Conference on Innovation and Entrepreneurship; 19-20 September; 2019 Kalamata, Greece; 2019. p. 336-344

[26] Idrisov GI, Knyaginin VN, Kudrin AL, Rozhkova ES. New technological revolution: Challenges and opportunities for Russia. Voprosy Ekonomiki. 2018; 4: 5-25.

[27] Edler J, Fagerberg J. Innovation policy: What. why. and how. Oxford Review of Economic Policy. 1917; 33: 2-23.

[28] Barney J. Firm resources and sustained competitive advantage. Journal of Management. 1991; 17: 99-120.

[29] Rumelt R P. Toward a strategic theory of the firm. In: Lamb R, editor. Competitive Strategic Management. New York: Prentice Hall. Englewood Cliffs. 1984; p. 556-570.

[30] Thomä J, Bizer K. To protect or not to protect? Modes of appropriability in the small enterprise sector. Research Policy. 2013; 42: p. 35-49.

[31] Schumpeter J, Capitalism. Socialism and Democracy. London:George Allen & Unwin; 1942.

[32] Earl P, Potts J. The market for preferences. Cambridge Journal of Economics. 2004; 28; p. 619-633.

[33] Schot J, Geels F W. Niches in evolutionary theories of technical change. A critical survey of the literature. Journal of Evolutionary Economics. 2007; 17: p. 605-622.

[34] Golichenko O. A path to leadership of innovation for a developing country. In: Proceedings of the 13th European Conference on Innovation and Entrepreneurship; 20-21 September 2018; Aveiro. Portugal. 2018. p. 273-283

[35] Dopfer K. The economic agent as rule maker and rule user: *Homo sapiens* oeconomicus. Journal of Evolutionary Economics. 2004; 14: p. 177-195.

[36] Gould S J. The Structure of Evolutionary Thought. Cambridge: Harvard University Press; 2002.

[37] Wilson. C. Up-scaling. formative phases. and learning in the historical diffusion of energy technologies. Energy Policy. 2012; 50: p. 81-94.

[38] Arthur W B. Competing technologies, increasing returns, and lock-in by historical events. The Economic Journal. 1989; 99: p. 116-131.

[39] Gould S J. Ever since Darwin: Reflections in Natural History. Harmondsworth. Middlesex: Penguin; 1991.

Chapter 4

The Role of Banks for the Transition to Circular Economy

Virginia Zhelyazkova

Abstract

The financial system as a whole—in Europe the banks, in the USA mainly the stock exchanges—is oriented mainly towards financing the linear economy. It is the dominant economic model; the production cycles, hence the business cycles of the individual industries and products, are well known. This ensures relative predictability of the amount of expected profits they generate, and it gives the necessary degree of probability for the financial markets for the return on investment. In order for banks to provide the much-needed resource for the transformation of the linear economy into a circular one, they must undergo a major transformation. It is multi-layered and, of course, has many specific characteristics. As banks definitely play a dominant role in Europe's financing of the economy, the analysis in this paper will focus on them. Certain main trends will be presented, related to circular economy and directing to the future development of individual segments within their framework.

Keywords: circular economy, linear economy, environmental risk in lending, green bank, transformation

1. Introduction

Banks are among the main sources of capital for the activities of companies. Their role in the development of modern economic systems is leading—they redistribute funds between individual economic entities. To a large extent, they are in charge of granting credit resources and determining the conditions for financing. That is why the policies that banks adopt in this area are extremely important when it comes to the transition from a linear to a circular model of the economy.

In general, the following problem areas can be outlined for the banks that will be addressed in this paper:

- Regulatory—like all for-profit organizations, banks will naturally continue to finance the linear economy in all possible forms when it is profitable for them. In order to start restricting access to finance for activities that run counter to the circular economy, banks must be subject to at least two types of "incentives":
    - pressure from the regulatory authorities, i.e. by the state through the central bank;

  - pressure from the regulatory authorities on their customers (specific economic entities) to transform their activities. This pressure could take the form of various barriers to linear production, fines and other sanctions, which together increase the risk of losses for banks because they could not, for example, collect receivables from their customers whose products no longer have a market (due to a ban by the state on trading with the products they produce, for example, as they are the result of linear production);

- Management—the need for bank management to realize the necessity for change. This is a prerequisite for the implementation of any policy, especially when it leads to a sharp turn from the traditional way of functioning. Also, some studies emphasize that good corporate governance can lead to improved investment yield for the customers [1]. However, this awareness will emerge naturally under the pressure of change from regulators. In the context of such awareness, bank management will be able to play its key role in identifying the new products and services that institutions will start offering to individuals in the context of the transformation to circular economy. Banking activity is also associated with a number of risks inherent to the economies as a whole [2] and banks will have to start acknowledging and actively managing the whole new array of risks that are emerging, in particular the environmental and climate ones. This will take place again under regulatory pressure;

- Building and maintaining internal administrative capacity. Not only the management, but also the employees of the banks will have to acquire knowledge about the new features of circular production. This will be necessary because circular production has a different cycle and features in terms of its economic dimensions—costs, revenues, profits, life expectancy of products, etc. All these dimensions both individually and collectively affect the various characteristics of bank products—collateral values, exposure at default, probability of default, loss given default, expected losses and many others. Hence the necessity for having knowledge about them and deeper understanding about the way they interact among themselves, and when impacting bank ratios. It must be acknowledged that building such internal capacity requires time and has proven to be a lengthy process. It is challenging for banks since they need to find experts who are capable of presenting in a catchy way to bank employees the interdisciplinary matters related to circular economy and its impact on banks. It is not impossible, though, such experts to be identified, since the interest in the subject of circular economy has been growing in recent years.

2. Emergence of the concept of circular economy

Over the past hundred years, an interesting pattern has been observed. On the one hand, the consumption of resources worldwide has been increasing, but on the other hand, the way in which these resources are consumed is clearly proving its inefficiency. The inefficiency can be outlined in two spheres, which leads to two main defects of the linear model.

First, there is an uneven consumption of resources—most of them are consumed in highly developed countries at the expense of developing countries, and secondly, there is an accumulation of huge amounts of waste that are not used after being disposed of. The current economic model is linear and follows the pattern: extraction of natural resources, processing into finished products and the consumption of the products, which ends with their disposal. According to a number of studies, the current linear economic cannot ensure the achievement of economic development by all countries in the world, as the available natural resources are insufficient for the purpose.

The circular model seeks to solve these two main defects of the linear model. The idea of this model draws inspiration from the way nature works, and in particular the individual biosystems. Just as each of them has its own cycle—birth, development, decline, death and rebirth, so do the individual systems within the economy.

Therefore, the life of a product should not end with its disposal in the form of waste that can no longer be used, but on the contrary—each product should be seen as an eternally existing set of materials, each of which, after the conditional end of the life of the given product, must be included in the creation of a new product. Thus, at some point in the future, society should reach a state where virtually no waste is disposed of, and all products are recycled or used in some way.

In order to gradually come to this point, it is not enough just to find ways to recycle individual types of goods, but to reduce the total amount of waste disposed of. In support of efforts in this direction, ways should be sought to prolong the life of products, to encourage their longer use, as well as to share the use of certain categories of goods, which would lead to a smaller number of goods in circulation.

It is difficult to determine exactly when and where the term "circular economy" itself has occurred. Today, "almost all international business operations are experiencing changes due to the pursuit of nature conservation" and efforts to make the transition from a linear to a circular model reflect this trend.

The term "circular economy" began to gain popularity in the 1970s, and gained popularity mainly due to several names.

The idea of circular material flows was first introduced in 1966 by Kenneth Bo-ulding in his study, "The Economics of the Coming Spaceship Earth". Later, the idea of circular economy began to be seriously researched and developed by the Swiss architect Walter Stahel. In 1976, in a report to the European Commission entitled "The Potential for Substituting Manpower for Energy", Walter Stahel and Genevieve Redey presented the concept of circular economy. In the report, they outline the main impacts that the transformation of the linear economy into a circular one will have on the creation of labor, conservation and optimization of the use of natural resources, control of nature pollution and economic efficiency. In 1982, the report was published as a book entitled "Jobs for Tomorrow: The Potential for Substituting Manpower for Energy" and its authors won the prestigious Mitchell Award.

Stahel's ideas have been further developed by Ellen MacArthur, a former world yacht record holder who founded an independent charity foundation of the same name in 2010 [3]. At the beginning of its activity, the foundation was supported by several powerful companies such as Renault, British Telecommunications, Cisco, etc., which provided funds for the implementation of the planned large-scale activities. One of the main goals of this foundation is to provoke a wide debate on the circular economy among the various economic schools, and thus the idea to gain wide popularity and gradually be adopted by governments around the world.

Two years after its establishment, in 2012, the foundation published a report, which outlined the prospects for the development of the world as a result of the transition from a linear model of the economy to a circular one. In the following year, 2013, this foundation, together with the consulting firm McKinsey, prepared and published a detailed report on circular economy and the opportunities that it offers to the consumer goods sector [4]. These reports has had a strong impact on public opinion, especially in Europe, and since 2015 the European Commission has launched an all-embracive agenda for the transition of the economy of the union from linear to a circular one, which already shows the presence of serious awareness among EU leaders on the issue. The concept of circular economy in EU has direct impact also on other financial institutions (insurers and pension funds) [5].

In practice, circular economy has functioned naturally from the very beginning of human activity. Technological progress made possible the extraction of huge quantities of raw materials, the creation of synthetic materials and the production of large number of goods at low prices. However, the quantity of goods has been enormously increasing, and subsequently it has turned out that some of these goods cannot be decomposed or reused in one way or another. In the process of production a number of environmentally harmful substances are released, it is necessary to build huge landfills, which in turn take over the disposed waste. As a result of these processes, the pressure on the environment increases enormously. Man is part of the biosphere and cannot be isolated from the processes that take place in it. Solving environmental problems is becoming a primary imperative of modern times.

From the middle of the twentieth century, when the shortcomings of the linear model became apparent, separate studies began to appear, as well as social movements that sought to define problems and propose solutions. This is how the concepts of eco-efficiency, systems thinking, the blue economy, industrial ecology, swing to swing and others emerged. What these separate theoretical concepts have in common is the idea of the need for transformation of the linear economic model, using examples from nature. Economy is a form of human activity, and man is an integral part of nature. It is therefore not possible for the systems he creates to function effectively under laws other than natural ones. Failure to take into account the effects of human activity on the environment, even if in the short term no serious consequences of financial nature are observed, in the medium term proves to be ineffective from an economic point of view. These theoretical concepts articulate precisely this basic feature of the linear economic model. Gradually, more and more countries around the world, led by the most developed ones, accept the need to change the model and begin to build strategies and policies in this direction.

3. Banks and circular economy

The transition from a linear to a circular model of the economy requires a number of changes in the way banks operate. This transition creates both opportunities and risks for them. A recent ING Bank study on this topic outlined the main opportunities and challenges for banks. In general, they can be linked to five main business models [6].

The first model aims at transforming production processes so that only raw materials from renewable sources or those that are subject to full recycling are used. In this way the waste will be eliminated and the depletion of natural resources will be stopped. Proponents of this model share the belief that this is the only way to move from a linear to a circular model of the economy.

The second business model concerns the re-use of the materials from which products are made to make new goods.

At the heart of the third model is the concept of extending the life cycle of products by repairing and improving them, as well as a result of additional efforts to advertise them on new markets. Extending the life of goods will not only delay their disposal in the form of waste, but will also generate profits from their sale, lease and use.

The fourth business model offers the replacement of the individual use of different goods with a collective one. For example, sharing cars, various devices, etc. This will eliminate the low efficiency inherent in the use of such goods, which when used by single individuals are often depreciated without being actually used long enough.

The fifth model offers a fundamental change in the way someone looks at goods: from an asset owned by its owner to a service that is used only when necessary. This will lead to a number of effects. On the one hand, the efficiency of the use of goods will increase. On the other hand, more people will have access to them. Third, as a result of more people using more goods, a number of ancillary markets will be created where other complementary goods and services will be offered.

As there is significant public interest in introducing different variants of the five circular models, the market for products and services related to them is generally expected to reach a net growth of between 1% and 4% in the next ten years. This is an opportunity for banks to offer their products and services and expand their customer base and market share. In addition, such a policy resonates with the intentions announced by more and more banks to support sustainable development. Research shows that customers who work in the field of sustainable development in one way or another are more innovative, demonstrate better financial results and have better credit ratings, which means lower credit risk for banks and greater security of investments. This is another reason why organizations need to stimulate innovative practices at workplace [7].

At the same time, financing of the circular economy poses a number of challenges for banks. First of all, due to the extension of the life of products, it is necessary to rethink the way of assessing the collaterals. This is naturally reflected in the risk assessment, especially the credit risk of the respective transaction and the client, and hence on all indicators relevant to the monitoring of credit risk, such as loss given default (LGD), exposure at default (EAD), probability of default (PD), and expected losses (EL).

Another important principle of circular economy related to the exploitation of goods for a longer than usual time, means not only that they need to have the functional characteristics for a longer life, but also that they need to actually circulate on the market. An example is Philips' policy to take medical equipment from its affluent customers after it has been exploited for some time and resell it on the secondary market, where there is demand from less solvent companies. Such actions are often undertaken after the equipment has been fully depreciated from an accounting point of view. This raises the question of depreciation rates for such equipment. If the company that buys it on the secondary market does so using loans where the equipment serves as collateral, the bank will have to evaluate it in some way.

Second, the tendency to prefer leased instead of owned products affects banks at least in two ways. On the one hand, they no longer have the possibility to accept the leased product as collateral for the loans, it remains the property of the company from which the bank's customer takes it for use. Therefore, banks need to rethink the model in which they finance such customers. On the other hand, using a leased item instead of buying it, actually expands the market for it, as more people can afford it.

The expansion of the market for the product in question theoretically leads to an expansion of the market for banks, but they will have to change their risk assessment schemes for this new category of customers. The expectations are that the customers who use leased goods in their main part will not be highly solvent. So banks will take additional risks when financing such clients. In addition, ownership of the commodity is unlikely to be transferred to the banks as collateral, and this will further increase the riskiness of such transactions.

Therefore, it can be said that the trend in the financing the circular model is characterized by a shift of focus from the importance of collateral to that of cash flows. Such a shift requires a complete change in the concept of banking and fundamental changes in banks' credit policies.

Third, the importance of the leasing form of financing will increase. Banks can play the role of leasing goods on a much larger scale than at present. Demand for leased goods will increase, as already mentioned, and this is an additional opportunity for banks. The challenges arising from the expansion of leasing portfolios both in terms of the types of goods offered on lease and the types of customers are related to the need to know the specifics of these goods, as well as the characteristics of customer behavior. The extension of the useful life of the goods will have to be reflected in the calculation of the risk of the clients in the leasing portfolio. On the other hand, here, as well as in the loan portfolio, banks will have to redefine their leasing policies, taking into account the extended life of goods and the relatively lower solvency of customers.

Fourth, due to changing consumer preferences on the one hand, and on the other hand, due to the growing number of regulatory requirements for business regarding its implications on the environment, banks will have to develop and integrate into their existing models for credit risk assessment, environmental risk assessment.

Monitoring the environmental risk in loan portfolios, including the leasing part, will gradually become imperative. The difficulties in this area are due to the lack of a uniform methodology for the assessment of environmental risk, which raises uncertainty that it can be correctly evaluated and unwillingness on the part of banks to start work in this direction.

Environmental risk management in real banking activities is key to banks' contribution to the development of the circular economy. As long as lending to companies that maintain the linear model and lack strategy and vision for change continues, it will be very difficult to achieve transition to a circular economy. For their part, banks are profit-oriented and this is natural—the pursuit of financial success is part of the rational thinking of every economic entity. Therefore, if there are no incentives for banks to refuse financing to highly profitable but environmentally harmful companies, they will not do so. Nor will they fund many innovative, inherently excellent ideas that support the circular model, but which are characterized by questionable, at least in the short term, profitability. Banks should not be blamed for this course of action and no change can be expected on their part without good reason.

At this stage, the picture from the point of view of banks looks as follows and this complicates the process of environmental risk management:

1. There are no regulatory requirements (Basel III, regulations of national banks) to impose on banks the obligation to monitor in detail the environmental risks associated with lending to companies. This immediately means that this activity remains in the sphere of the good will of the management of banks.

2. Banks wishing to implement an environmental risk management system face a lack of a unified methodology for doing so. At present, perhaps the most applied methodology is that of the European Bank for Reconstruction and Development (EBRD). It is clear and well developed. However, even when applied, many additional methodological issues naturally arise, stemming from the need to adapt it on the one hand to the specificities of national laws and industry classifications, and on the other hand to the specific characteristics of portfolios of individual banks.

3. A third problem, which, however, can hardly be avoided, even if there was a standardized and globally accepted methodology, is the purely technological, software integration of environmental risk assessment into the credit risk

assessment systems. This usually has to be the subject of a separate serious internal bank projects, which take a lot of resources and time, and which would be difficult to initiate, if there was no regulatory pressure to implement it.

Despite the declared desire of the countries (the European Union as a whole and each individual country as part of it, and this to a greater or lesser extent applies to all other countries in the world)—to change the model from linear to circular, at this point there are virtually no simplified and easy-to-apply tools to support this change.

The development of the five models related to the transition to circular economy, mentioned above, requires serious funding. In many cases, funding must take place before it is clear exactly what the market for a given product or service will be, whether there will be demand for it, whether consumers will want to change their habits and, if so, with what time lag in relation to the introduction of new products and services will this happen.

If we look, for example, at a model that describes the shift pf consumer preferences from buying a product and paying for it to leasing it needed—when could that happen? Can the transition be made for all goods at the same time, or will it take place for some goods as soon as there is the possibility of leasing, and for others it will take years of changing consumer habits? Undoubtedly, contrary to the theory of rational thinking of economic entities, it will turn out that for some groups of goods, especially those in the luxury segment, possession will continue to be a matter of prestige and customers will keep on paying for owning them.

These are important issues that require very serious consideration in order appropriate form of financing to be found for ventures aimed at implementing new business models. It would not be realistic to expect banks to readily take the risk of experimenting with financing activities for which they themselves cannot determine, at least to some extent, the future return. Without being able to determine the expected future return on a loan, it is difficult to calculate the most important parameters for credit risk management such as PD, EAD, LGD, and EL. Therefore, the governments must intervene at least at the initial stage of the transition to circular economy, standing behind the various new ventures.

The government support can be realized in the form of state guarantees and participation in various activities. If the state creates a guarantee fund for initiatives aimed at implementing one of the five business models related to circular economy, banks would provide the necessary credit resources to entrepreneurs. Some years afterwards, when experience is gained in such projects, the answers to some of the above questions will have been established and the transition to circular economy will have gained momentum, governments will be able to withdraw.

Therefore, it can be said that banks expect governments to take the initiative to be actively involved in financing the circular economy. However, governments have no reason to expect banks to take the first step based on purely market considerations. The uncertainty in the beginning of transitional periods is too great, and it is necessary to remember that banks are conservative institutions.

Environmental risk management is not just a passive activity, consisting of the application of a procedure in which various documents of the clients are considered, or in the calculation of scoring for them on the basis of exposure parameters and other indicators. It has also a proactive part, which consists not only in assessing the customer in terms of whether he meets the existing conditions and matches the existing product range in the bank, but in developing such products and services which will meet his new needs reflect his profile.

However, in order to create such products, serious work is needed inside the banks. The necessary level of expertise must be built, which includes knowledge of the latest market trends, customers' purchasing power, demand trends, and last but not least, the demographic characteristics of society. It should not be forgotten that young people are more likely to change their consumer habits. Middle-aged people, as well as retirees, are in most cases not among those ready to change their behavior. In order to create products that are aimed at protecting the environment in one way or another, and to find a market for these products, banks need to explore this whole range of problems, and perhaps many more, which at this stage cannot be foreseen.

4. Comprehensive environmental risk management and the green bank concept

In order for banks to contribute to the transition to circular economy, they themselves must be oriented towards it. When we talk about the environmental aspects of circular economy, at the micro level, this should mean for banks that they should be "green", in the sense that they should regard environmental protection as their philosophy and strategy. This coincides with the introduction of a comprehensive environmental risk management system in the banks—and this system not only covers internal resource consumption and monitoring of the level of environmental risk of loans after disbursement, but is proactive in the field of development of banking products and services aimed at preservation of the environment.

There are four levels (levels) of environmental risk management in banks [8].

The first level is related to the management of this part of environmental risk, which arises from the so-called direct effects of banking activity. These effects are the consequences of the day-to-day operations of the bank, for the needs of which it uses energy from various sources, paper, and water, generates waste, etc.

The second level builds on the first and also involves the development of environmental risk management policy in the core business of the bank, in the case of European banks, mainly in the field of corporate lending (in this level we include leasing, factoring and other forms of trade finance).

The third level covers the first two and extends environmental risk management through the development of appropriate products aimed at preservation of the environment, or, this is, as mentioned above, proactive risk management.

The fourth, highest level builds on the third and presupposes the orientation of the deposit policy to sources of resources that have a proven positive attitude towards the environment.

While many banks have already reached the first and second levels, the third (especially in the area of creation of a comprehensive product policy aimed at preservation of the environment, and not just the sporadic appearance of some "exotic" banking products) and the fourth belong entirely to the future.

The International Banking Community, represented by the United Nations Environmental Program Finance Initiative (UNEP FI), recognizes the need for a fundamental change in banks' approach to the economy. In the context of this way of thinking is the Positive Impact Manifesto adopted by this organization in May 2016. It declares that banks must use their unique position as intermediaries between the real economy and capital markets and begin to reorient their business models to financing sustainable development, an integral part of which is environmental protection. The aim of this change must be the realization of an overall positive impact of their activities, which in turn is defined as "leading to a positive impact on the economy, society and the environment, after proper consideration and minimization of all negative impacts."

A recent study, initiated by UNEP FI by the Institute for Sustainable Leadership at the University of Cambridge, outlines the main reasons why banks urgently need to take action to refocus from conventional e financing to supporting the circular model through environmental risk management at all levels [9].

First of all, it is pointed out that environmental risks are increasing both in number and intensity. As a result, there is an increasing interaction between them and other socio-economic trends, which already in their entirety affect the financial stability in various places.

Secondly, a number of indirect effects of increasing environmental risks also appear. Indirect effects are related to the public response to these risks, which is often transferred to certain regulatory initiatives. All this affects the environment in which banks operate and the success of their business models.

Third, environmental risks are beginning to manifest themselves in an increasingly complex way. This is due to several reasons:

- the growing connection between the different types of environmental risks;
- uncertainty about the time horizons in which these risks will manifest themselves, their frequency and intensity;
- development of the manifestation of some of the environmental risks and the creation of various interdependencies between them over time.

A good example that illustrates these three features is the consequences observed in the United States in the 1930s as a result of the application of a number of unsuccessful agricultural practices over large areas over the previous 100 years. Dust storms, which are formed due to the disturbance of the ecological balance and the deterioration of the quality of the soils, practically ruin the economy of entire agricultural regions. Subsequently, an economic crisis ensued, leading to massive losses for farmers' creditor banks.

The importance of these risks increasingly necessitates serious regulatory action. In this direction is the study of the University of Cambridge in conjunction with UNEP FI, led by Prof. K. Alexander of the University of Zurich. The thesis defended in this study is that in all financial crises banks suffer serious losses from the underestimation of the various risks they face in their activities and urgently need to take measures to include the assessment of environmental risk in banking regulations such as those of the Basel III framework.

At this stage, Basel III requires Pillar I banks to include an assessment of environmental risks in assessing the extent to which they are exposed to credit and operational risk. In particular, paragraph № 510 of Basel II and Basel III requires banks to monitor the risk of environmental liability for collateral. It is assumed that in order to be able to carry out such monitoring, banks must undertake to carry out (including hired consultants) thorough collateral checks of individual cases of transactions with a high environmental risk. However, the requirements for monitoring the environmental risk defined in this way remain desirable and no specific requirements and rules have been set in this regard. They mainly concern the environmental risk that would arise in individual transactions (lending), but do not consider its impact in a broader, macroprudential plan.

The review of the state of regulations in relation to environmental risk management in the banking system, presented in the study of the University of Cambridge, shows that in some countries around the world national regulations in this direction are quite advanced. Of particular interest are the examples of China, Brazil and Peru.

It can be said that the Chinese Banking Regulatory Commission acts to support the development of the third level of environmental risk management—proactive—by financing environmentally sustainable projects and requiring banks in their contracts with customers to set compliance clauses of certain environmental standards. This policy was launched in 2007 by the Banking Commission and the Ministry of the Environment in the form of a document entitled "Green Credit Policies". In 2012, the publication of "Guidelines for Green Lending", consisting of instructions to banks on how to implement the policy and compliance with credit requirements followed.

The Commission oblige banks to collect and pass on statistics on the financing they provide to companies in the construction and transport sectors. Through these statistics, the Commission, together with the Ministry of Environment, monitors the country's progress in achieving national environmental goals. Another interesting feature of the requirements introduced in 2012 to banks is the obligation to monitor whether their customers comply with environmental standards and laws and to sanction them in case of violations by making changes to loan agreements. The main sanction that is applied is a requirement for early repayment of loans, in the event that after establishing the violation and subsequent warning, the client does not take corrective action within the period specified by the bank. In case of proven non-compliance with the environmental legislation, a client may be denied a loan at all. Another measure aimed at orienting companies to environmental projects is the granting of loans for non-environmentally friendly projects at higher interest rates, as well as generally difficult access to financing from banks.

The Commission obliges banks to incorporate the assessment and monitoring of environmental risk in their overall activity, which includes auditing the data.

Brazil is the next example of proactive environmental risk management by banks as a result of regulatory requirements, but China is ahead in this regard. In 2014, the Central Bank of Brazil issued a guidance document on the application of the Basel III Pillar II requirements for asset reviews and process assessments in banks, requiring them to take into account the extent to which they are exposed to environmental and social risk. This document also requires banks to prepare and disclose environmental and social risk reporting in their portfolios, dressing it in the form of following the Basel III Pillar III regulations. Penalties are envisaged for non-compliance with this requirement.

The approach of the Financial Regulator in Peru differs from that of the Chinese and Brazilian central banks. It definitely deserves to be defined as innovative and aimed at creating a lasting culture of assessment and management of environmental and social risk both among banks and the corporate world in the country. The Peruvian regulator requires from banks to prepare a report on the environmental and social risks associated with the project before funding is granted. Only after the report is considered together, of course, with the other documents of the company applying for a loan, and after the bank is convinced that the risks are acceptable, can the process of financing start. According to a 2014 report by the director of the Peruvian regulator, Dr. Daniel Szydlowski, this requirement has led to a significant improvement in the overall financial risk in Peru and the number of bad loans has decreased significantly [Ibidem].

5. Conclusion

Unlike China, Brazil and Peru, the most developed countries in the world have not created regulations to encourage proactive management of environmental risk and hence—lending to projects aimed at protecting the environment and thus encouraging the transition to circular economy.

It is necessary to think not only about the manifestation of environmental risks at the transaction level or at individual client level, but also at macro level in order to be able to make a comprehensive assessment of how and in what way the banking system is exposed to them and therefore to what extent it contributes to the transformation of the linear model into circular one.

In addition to regulations such as the Basel III rules, Prof. K. Alexander and his team propose to consider ways for the state to support projects aimed at protecting the environment with monetary policy instruments. Since the protection of the environment should be state priority, then it is natural for it to purposefully allocate money in this direction, with banks playing the role of intermediaries.

This idea provoked mixed reactions from representatives of individual countries during its discussion in the framework of the study that UNEP FI issued. For some countries, such policy is appropriate, while for others it seems to have the potential for destabilization. For example, China has taken a similar approach, while Brazil and Peru fear that declaring some kind of quantitative easing to help the environment could be interpreted by capital market investors as a sign of volatile monetary policy. The world is already witnessing an experiment by the Lebanese Central Bank, which by Decree № 7835 decided to grant special liquidity to the country's banks to be used for disbursing lending to various green investment activities.

The monetary policy approach to stimulate green lending is generally more complex and unlikely to be easily adopted by most central banks around the world, mainly because of the divergent market reactions that follow each market quantitative easing.

In a nutshell, it can be said that in the field of assessment, monitoring and disclosure of information on environmental risk at this stage there is no standardization internationally, as well as mandatory requirements for banks to monitor this risk. The existing requirements in Basel III are vague and general. The way they are formulated allows banks to circumvent the monitoring of environmental risk, giving priority to clear financial benefits for themselves in financing various transactions.

Therefore, the current state of regulations in most of the world encourages the overlooking of environmental risks. This is due to the lack of sufficient understanding of the problem at macro level. Proof of this are the examples of China, Brazil and Peru. These countries have specific requirements for banks in terms of environmental risk management and the results of this policy, as shown by the practice in Peru, are encouraging. The Chinese authorities, on the other hand, have come to a profound understanding that the economy of this huge developing country would not have a sustainable future if the imperatives of the environment were ignored. This has pushed them from now on to set strict requirements for both banks and companies from all sectors of the economy to comply with environmental legislation. Serious sanctions, which are provided in cases of violations, are a good enough incentive for market participants to follow the laws. In this way, as in Peru and Brazil, China is working to build a holistic culture in a society centered on environmental protection.

Author details

Virginia Zhelyazkova
VUZF University, Sofia, Bulgaria

*Address all correspondence to: vzhelyazkova@vuzf.bg;
virginia.zhelyazkova@gmail.com

References

[1] Dimitrov St., The PEPP Regulation and its influence on the Bulgarian market of insurance, p.4, 13th Young researchers scientific conference, ISBN: 978-954-8590-45-7, VUZF Publishing House St. Grigorii Bogoslov, Sofia, 2017

[2] Angelov. R. Mergers and Acquisition in the Banking Sector. Theory and Practice of Control. VUZF University, 2020, ISBN978-954-8590-77-8, p. 12 (in Bulgarian)

[3] Interview: Ellen MacArthur - Voyage of self-discovery, The Scotsman, http://www.scotsman.com/lifestyle/interview-ellen-macarthur-voyage-of-self-discovery-1-808060

[4] Towards the Circular Economy. Opportunities for the Consumer Goods Sector, McKinsey, 2013

[5] Dimitrov, St. (2020). "Integration of Environmental, Social and Governance Principles in Pension Funds and Insurance Companies' Activities", p.18, Money and Culture Magazine, vol. 1, 2020, ISSN 2683-0965, pp. 13 - 25, https://sites.google.com/vuzf.bg/money-and-culture/202

[6] Rethinking Finance in a Circular Economy. Financial implications of circular business models. ING. 2015

[7] Lazarova, T. Innovative Human Recourse Management. VUZF University, ISBN 978-954-8590-50-1, p. 13, (in Bulgarian)

[8] Zhelyazkova, V. Circular Economy. Financial Aspects. VUZF University, 2017, ISBN 978-954-8590-42-6 9, (in Bulgarian)

[9] Stability and Sustainability in Banking Reform. Are Environmental Risks Missing in Basel III? 2014 University of Cambridge Institute for Sustainability Leadership

Chapter 5

Meeting the Needs of Fourth Industrial Revolution (4IR) in Entrepreneurial Education in Malaysia: The Government's Role

Hanim Kamaruddin, Rosilah Hassan, Norasmah Othman, Wan Mimi Diyana Wan Zaki and Sarmila Md Sum

Abstract

Entrepreneurship education holds great value for all students of science, technology, mission work, social work, healthcare, and education. It also serves as a great incubator for the types of creative, innovative ideas of our students and the global needs in the 21st century where combining entrepreneurship syllabus and exposure of the fourth industrial revolution is essential. This study explores the Fourth Industrial Revolution (4IR) as an opportunity to change models of innovation-driven entrepreneurship for the better, and create an environment that makes entrepreneurship more inclusive, while maximizing the Fourth Industrial Revolution's benefits to the society and minimizing the risks that come with it. The role of Malaysian government in enhancing entrepreneurial education must therefore recognize the fourth industrial evolution and its impacts that must be compatible with Malaysia's industry policy. Promotion of entrepreneurial experimentation within an appropriate entrepreneurial education ecosystem will provide entrepreneurs with smart government support that invests in entrepreneurial skills in Malaysia. This article assesses (i) fourth industrial revolution impact on entrepreneurial education; (ii) new expectations arising from impacts of fourth industrial evolution in Malaysia: method in teaching and learning; (iii) government's role in supporting entrepreneurship education and finally (iv) entrepreneurial education reforms in Malaysia.

Keywords: Malaysia, entrepreneur, education, government, 4IR

1. Introduction

Recognizing the importance of entrepreneurship education in inspiring entrepreneurship development and the economy, Malaysia Ministry of Higher Education (MOHE) has taken the initiative by making entrepreneurship subjects compulsory to all students at all universities [1]. The students are encouraged to take part in the entrepreneurship activities at their respective universities in order to develop the entrepreneurial attitudes and mind-set. The advancement in technology revolution is transforming method of educating through the usage of digital application that will eventually discard the traditional of concept time-honored classroom teaching.

The 4IR will experience a combination of technologies that distort the lines between the physical, digital and biological spheres. It is, indeed, built upon the Third Industrial Revolution known as the digital revolution since the 1950's as revealed by Smelser [2]. The Fourth Industrial Revolution can be referred as the current proliferation of technological advancements driven by connectivity, speed, breadth and depth of transformation. It is reinforced by the digital economy that emphasize some rapid advances in emergent innovation areas like artificial intelligence (AI), internet of things (IoT), robots, block chain, 3D printing and cloud computing that are transforming industries and societies across the world. AI is best described as a wide field of study with applications to many disciplines and various subfields.

With the emergence and availability of computers or machines, their capability to perform various tasks have grown and developed at a quick pace. Specialists and professionals have developed the power of computer systems to be applied in diverse working domains that focused on increasing speed and reducing its size with respect to time. Applications of AI has shown a growing and advanced applications in various fields such as gaming, natural language processing (NLP), expert system, vision system, speech recognition, handwriting recognition and intelligent robot.

The ten (10) major Fourth Industrial Revolution (4IR) technologies revealed at World Economic Forum in 2017 with potential to be the most influential over the next decade whereby their impacts are not limited to shaping industry and businesses worldwide but also in helping to secure and enhance the planet's sustainability. This suggests the importance of environmental sustainability technologies that will attribute to the broader social challenges of the 21st century. The fast emergence of 4IR and its impacts must therefore translate to new implementation in Education 4.0 that focuses on empowering education to adapt to new challenges in teaching and content that creates and motivates innovation in technology.

2. New expectations arising from impacts of 4IR in Malaysia

Nowadays, all graduates face a world transform by technology, in which the internet and social media create different opportunities and challenges for formal education systems. As students consider life after graduation, the universities are facing questions about their own destiny especially in ensuring graduates are fully employed. In the era of fourth industrial age, students require to acquire certain skills that are not exactly the same as the skills that were required in the previous era (third industrial revolution) where information technology was the key driver. The skills emphasis needs to be shifted towards imparting of complex, problem solving skills: creative skills and social skills including management, leadership, change management, collaboration, critical thinking, curiosity and risk taking, communication, marketing and sales [3]. Further, emotional intelligence, judgment, negotiation, decision making, cognitive flexibility, as well as knowledge production are also skills that are required for the new era entrepreneurship.

With this development, many changes need to occur in the education system. For example, changes need to be made in the curriculum of courses offered in universities and teaching methods used by the lecturers. However, the goal of higher education institution such as to ensure quality of learning via teaching, to enable the students to get the latest knowledge through exploratory research, and to sustain the development of societies by means of service will remain.

One of the main objectives of every higher institution is to educate the youth. Therefore, it is necessary to implement appropriate teaching strategies or method and to organize work in a way that foster learning. This has implication on better learning experience and lifelong learning attitude. The changes that is expected to occur in the Malaysian Higher Education System are changes in teaching and learning methods. For instance, the implementation of massive open online courses (MOOCs) has been introduced in 2014. According to Mohamed Amin [4], teaching in the classroom can no longer remain conventional if universities want to produce competitive, innovative and creative graduates. He added, those born in the era of mobile computing, which he called Generation Z, are skilled in sharing information through social media and are interested in learning new things online. Therefore, educators need to create teaching and learning contents which can stimulate their learning experience.

The use of MOOCs in teaching and learning has also been identified as beneficial in the education system. Amongst the benefits that have been identified are:

i. Will allow higher institutions to decrease the cost of creating and delivering programs without compromising quality.

ii. can reach a much broader audience student – of all ages anywhere in the country via an internet connection will now be able to access high quality courses even if there are not currently enrolled at higher learning institutions.

iii. Will allow higher learning institutions to quickly augment their programs with international courses content and/or add new courses which they could not previously provide.

Massive open online courses, or MOOCs, have been regarded as a dominant force in the transformation of pedagogy. Universiti Kebangsaan Malaysia (UKM) has launched its own version of MOOCs and actively used as one of the methods in teaching and learning. In 2016, a total of 122,021 students have registered for the UKM courses and as for 2018, UKM plans to add more courses uses MOOCs platform.

3. Malaysian government's role

The role of Malaysian government in preparing the future generation with entrepreneurial skills and mindsets has made some headway throughout the last decade with the establishment of the Higher Education Entrepreneurship Development Policy in 2010. This significant policy addressing six (6) core areas creates entrepreneurial values and cultures amongst students or graduates in the Higher Learning Institutions (HEI's) by alleviating the development of entrepreneurial programs into a more defined, holistic and well organized curriculum to produce graduates with heightened entrepreneurial attributes and thinking skills. The government envisages an increase in the number of entrepreneurs amongst the graduates to stimulate economic transformation towards a high-income nation. Hence, several marked achievements can be traced including:

1. Nineteen (19) Higher Education Institutions (HEIs) in Malaysia have introduced entrepreneurial education as a compulsory subject [5] that are Universiti Kebangsaan Malaysia, Universiti Teknologi MARA, Universiti Putra Malaysia, Universiti Malaya, Universiti Islam Antarabangsa, Universiti Sains Islam Malaysia, Universiti Malaysia Sabah, Universiti Malaysia Sarawak, Universiti

Malaysia Kelantan, Universiti Teknologi Malaysia, Universiti Teknologi Hussein Onn, Universiti Sains Malaysia, Universiti Malaysia Perlis, Universiti Malaysia Pahang, Universiti Utara Malaysia, Universiti Sultan Zainal Abidin, Universiti Perguruan Sultan Idris, Universiti Teknikal Melaka and Universiti Malaysia Terengganu.

2. Several thrusts in the Strategic Plan on Entrepreneurship Development in Higher Education (2013–2105) have been successful [6] which include establishing the Entrepreneurship Centre in every HEI, providing holistic and well-planned entrepreneurial education and programmes, enhancing the competency of HEI's entrepreneurship trainers and facilitators, and to increase the effect of the implementation of HEI's entrepreneurial education and development.

3. Various programs to stimulate entrepreneurial spirits and increase knowledge and skills such as 1Malaysia Entrepreneur (1MET), Program Usahawan Bimbing Usahawan, Business Design Workshop and Business Facilitator, Graduate Entrepreneur Scheme (SIS), Program Galakan Perniagaan and Program Pembudayaan Keusahawanan (INSKEN 2015), MSC Malaysia, Meet Your Experts (ER360), Majlis Amanah Rakyat, Small Medium Enterprise (SME) Corp Malaysia, Ministry of Domestic Trade, Cooperatives and Consumerism (KDNKK) and Perbadanan Nasional Berhad (PNS), Satu Daerah Satu Industri program (SDSI), Youth and Entrepreneurship Program (Business and Agriculture Business), Economic Transformation Program and Automotive Workshop Modernization or ATOM.

4. The establishment of Malaysian Global Innovation and Creativity Center (MAGIC), an entrepreneurial entity, formed by the Malaysian government in 2014 to develop dynamic entrepreneurs with high endurance equipped to take up challenges and make impact at regional and global stage.

5. The government provides micro-credit facilities through TEKUN Nasional and Amanah Ikhtiar Malaysia (AIM) to manage the micro-credit funds in tandem with entrepreneurship training to build women and youths' ability in finance, business plan preparation, marketing and promotion.

6. Women Entrepreneurship Incubator (I-KeuNITA) was introduced to harness women's skills training in micro enterprises providing intensive skills training and entrepreneurship assistance for low-income women in the field of sewing, beauty therapy, commercial cooking, crafts, childcare, and tour services. In addition, the Ministry of Women, Family and Community Development holds a Skills Training for Single Mothers (I-KIT) to encourage generation of income for single mothers [7].

Malaysia appears to be on the right track to ensure that transformation to a high-income nation by 2020 and beyond is attained. In that regard, the *Vision 2020* plan for the future of Malaysia between 2020 and 2050 needs to be put in place adapting to changes brought forth by 4IR. Hence, the universities having a serious role shall need to produce real future talents equipped with technological digital know how that must be supported with government's initiatives. It is invoked that future jobs require a new institutional approach that encourages universal skillset that complements significant changes that are coming quickly with a mix of both social skills and technical skills. A few examples of direction higher tertiary education employed in the US and UK universities towards that objective include:

i. Tulane University where targeted curriculum focuses around mission based and cross disciplinary learning that blends science and technology studies with entrepreneurship studies. The Bioinnovation PhD Programme trains students across the university's science, engineering, medicine, law and business faculties and supplements that academic breadth with 'real-world' support of the US FDA and New Orleans Bioinnovation Center [8].

ii. Cambridge University's Institute for Manufacturing offers a cross disciplinary collection of expertise in management, engineering, technology and policy relating to manufacturing.

iii. Stanford 2025 and Georgia Tech have taken steps to ensure life-long learning through online education is readily available where increasingly, the 3–4 year undergraduate degrees is deemed outdated. Thus, continuous learning is necessary to suit changing jobs and technologies to rapidly meet with the needs of a new technological revolution.

In Malaysia, a number of initiatives have developed across the higher learning institutions including the usage of Massive Open Online Courses (MOOC) that is seen as a progress from campus-based university education towards an online education.

After analyzing the future needs of the job market taking into consideration the fusion of digital and biological impact of 4IR, the Malaysia's Higher Education Ministry has prepared a framework, known as Education 4.0 Framework, to ensure that the higher education institutions are equipped for the challenges and demands of the 4IR. This move is a critical step in allowing for promising and future directions to create initiatives in local academic world to best safeguard against the certainty of unprecedented future 4IR will create for students and future graduates.

Hence, the role of Malaysian government is intensified as it has to ensure that the demands of 4IR can be fulfilled by an education system that is able to produce graduates with efficiency in technological expertise and humanistic issues.

4. Entrepreneurial education reforms

The [9] (MEB) (Higher Education) has integrated factors to tackle the uncertainty of the 4IR to produce holistic, balanced entrepreneurial graduates who can adapt and cater to newly created jobs that are yet to exist. Thus, the Ministry recognizes that the education system needs to keep abreast with global trends such as disruptive technologies, the Internet of Things and the automation of work knowledge. Hence, the MEB is constructed on five aspirations which are access, quality, equity, unity and efficiency that is further strengthened by its foundation for a balanced student emphasizing on six primary attributes. These attributes include ethics and spirituality, leadership skills, national identity, language proficiency, thinking skills and knowledge that can be instilled entrepreneurial mindset of graduates that places equal value on technical training. In order to achieve these aspirations, the MEB lays out 10 SHIFTS (see **Figure 1**) that will stimulate performance towards achieving excellence in the higher education system through three (3) phases beginning from 2015, 2016–2020 and finally in 2021–2025. The first four Shifts aim for outcomes from main stakeholders in our HE education system while another six Shifts focus on enablers in the HE ecosystem namely financial stability, empowered government, innovation ecosystem, global prominence, globalized

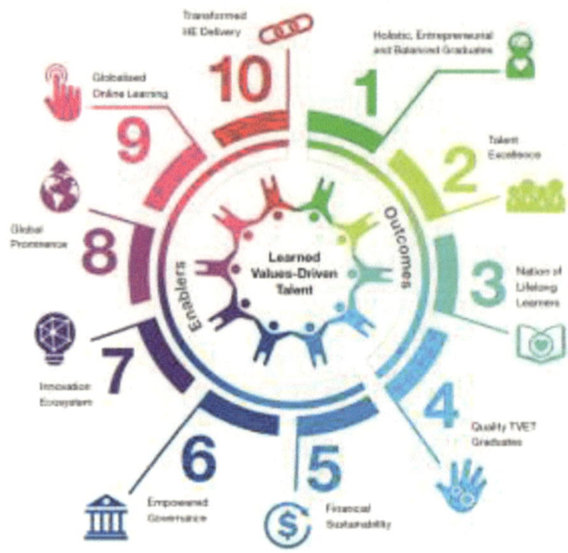

Figure 1.
The 10 SHIFTS. Source: [9].

online learning and transformed HE delivery. The Higher Education Ministry expects the transformation to be gained in the long term, but impact and changes will be visible in the short term building on future excellence.

With the emergence of 4IR, Malaysia has taken a much-needed educational strategy to introduce new methods to produce students to meet the demands of the new Revolution that must be powered by character building, higher order of thinking, multiple intelligences and soft skills. Various initiatives were undertaken that include the application of iCGPA which assesses students on their participation in co-curricular, social and voluntary activities, 2u2i Programme and the CEO @ Faculty Programme. In a more micro level initiative, universities in Malaysia are encouraged to give emphasis on data analytic skills for students across disciplines on top of the entrepreneurial skills. This effort is to adhere to the rapid development of processing power and availability of big data that are seen becoming one of the distortions to the entrepreneurial strategy. Hence, besides entrepreneurial skills, students need to have the ability to manage and take advantage of the data to come out with the best information for business decision particularly on the trend of the market and the availability of the supplier. In UKM, apart from offering the subject of Fundamentals of Entrepreneurship and Innovation [10, 11], the university is also offering Management and Data Analytic as compulsory subject to all the students to address method for managing, mining and analyzing big dataset.

It is further envisaged that in order to meet the challenges of the 4IR, several factors are required to enhance the education system including entrepreneurial curriculum content that are:

i. Application of Heutagogy which is "*the study of self-determined learning that attempts to challenge some ideas about teaching and learning that still prevail in teacher centered learning and the need for, as Bill Ford (1997) eloquently puts it 'knowledge sharing' rather than 'knowledge hoarding'. In this respect heutagogy looks to the future in which knowing how to learn will be a fundamental skill given the pace of innovation and the changing structure of communities and workplaces*".

Figure 2.
The 21st century curriculum for MyHE 4.0. Source: Datin Paduka and Tapsir [12].

ii. Delivery of Higher Education that asserts gamification, and on demand learning methods such as inverted classroom and blended learning.

iii. Curriculum Content which amplifies the need for balanced values of ethics and morality and knowledge and skills (**Figure 2**).

iv. Translational research which encompasses transdisciplinary collaborations, crowd sourcing, web of co-laboratories, quadruple helix innovation, a symbiosis of learning, research and collaborations and guided by human based research ethics.

The MOHE has realized 4IR is opening vast opportunities to on-line or e-commerce businesses which includes the Business to business (B2B), Business to Customer (B2C) and even Customer to Customer (C2C) business activities. In order to equip the current entrepreneurship education content, collaboration with the world e-commerce giant Ali-Baba Group Ltd., for example, was initiated with MOHE to participate in the Global E-Commerce Talent (GET) training program that provides lecturers and students of higher education with competitive skills required in the global e-commerce industry. It is the intent of the MOHE that with the e-commerce skills provided, the higher education in Malaysia would be able to develop more entrepreneur talent with new business model that benefits from 4IR that creates a platform to heighten connectivity in the existing entrepreneurial eco-system.

Hence, it is suffice to state that presently educational system in Malaysia is bracing for new paradigm shift or at a lesser extent enhancing the existing methods to ensure that entrepreneurial learning content is aligned with impacts of 4IR. Although the Education 4.0 Framework that address the issues and challenges of 4IR is yet to be realized, it is an evidence that the Malaysian government has quickly taken up the role to explore the impacts of 4IR to redesign the curriculum content at the higher learning institutions.

5. Conclusion

The business of higher education institutions remains unchanged in Malaysia since the establishment of the University of Malaya in 1949, however, students still assemble at a scheduled time and venue to listen to the wisdom and teachings by scholars. Given the fourth industrial revolution, a new form of university is emerging that implements teaching, research and service in an unconventional approach.

This version of university education is interdisciplinary and multi-disciplinary where methods of learning and teaching is conducted in virtual classrooms. Hence, the experience of learning is highly enhanced with the usage of technology and data management. Hence, all stakeholders especially the government needs to ensure that all tools and initiatives are well placed in all educational institutions to meet all the impacts of 4IR and benefits a potential entrepreneur graduate may gain from the new revolution.

Acknowledgements

This research is funded by National Higher Education Research Institute (IPPTN) under CLMV Research Grant – Executing UKM Entrepreneurship Education syllabus on Cambodian University (Code GG-2016-004) and FRGS/1/2018/TK04/UKM/02/07.

Author details

Hanim Kamaruddin*, Rosilah Hassan, Norasmah Othman, Wan Mimi Diyana Wan Zaki and Sarmila Md Sum
Universiti Kebangsaan Malaysia, UKM, 43600 Bangi, Selangor Darul Ehsan, Malaysia

*Address all correspondence to: hanim@ukm.edu.my

References

[1] Hardy Loh Rahim, Mohd Ali Bahari Abdul Kadir, Zanariah Zainal Abidin, Junainah Junid, Laila Mohd Kamaruddin, Noor Faizah Mohd Lajin, Siti Zahrah Buyong, and Adlan Ahmad Bakri, 2015. Entrepreneurship Education In Malaysia: A Critical Review, Journal of Technology Management and Business (ISSN: 2289-7224) Vol 02, No 02, 2015.

[2] Smelser NJ. Social Change in the Industrial Revolution: An Application of Theory to the British Cotton Industry. Routledge; 2013

[3] Naude W. Entreprenuership, Education and the Fourth Industrial Revolution in Africa. IZA Insitute of Labor Economic, Germany: Discussion paper series; 2017

[4] Mohamed Amin Embi, 2016. 35 Kursus Massive Open Online Courses (MOOC) baharu untuk pembelajaran sesi akademik 2016/2017.http://www.ukm.my/news/Latest_News/new-teaching-and-learning-method-for-generation-z/. Accessed 24 Jan 2019.

[5] Yussof B, Zainol FA & Ibrahim B 2015. Entrepreneurship Education in Malaysia's Public Institutions of Higher Learning—A Review of the Current Practices, International Education Studies. Volume 8, No. 1.

[6] Shamsudin SFFAAM, Nawi NBC, Nasir NABM, Zakaria MNB. Policies and practices for entrepreneurial education: The Malaysian experience. The Journal of Developing Areas. 2016;**50**(5):307-316

[7] Mutalib RA, Arshad R, Ismail NSA, Ahmad Z. Women and entrepreneurship: An overview of women entrepreneurship programs in Malaysia, JGD vol. 11. Special Issue on Social Entrepreneurship. 2015:15-28

[8] R. May Lee, Kendall, M. and Simmons, T, 2017, https://www.weforum.org/agenda/2017/10/to-train-tomorrow-s-leaders-universities-need-again-to-teach-universal-skillsets/. Accessed 23 December 2017.

[9] Malaysia Education Blueprint 2015-2025 (Higher Education), Ministry of Education, Malaysia

[10] Hassan R, Zaki WMDW, Kamaruddin H, Othman N, Sarmila MS. Fostering entrepreneurship foundation. Nurturing Innovation and Creativity in UKM Students, 7th International Conference on Global Social Entrepreneurship. 2016:43-50

[11] Rosilah Hassan, Wan Mimi Diyana Wan Zaki, Hanim Kamaruddin, Norasmah Othman, Sarmila Md Sum, Zulkifli Mohamad, 2017, Entrepreneurship Education in UKM: Essential Skills for first - Years Students, Leadership, innovation and entrepreneurship as driving forces of the global economy: Proceedings of the 2016 international conference on leadership, innovation and entrepreneurship (ICLIE), p 675-685.

[12] Datin Paduka IR, Siti Hamisah Tapsir, 2017, Keynote Speaker in University Presidential forum 2017, http://www.utm.my/upf/utm-university-presidents-forum-2017/. Accessed 30 January 2019.

Section 3

Opportunity and Future of Circular Economy Development

Chapter 6

Responding to Changes in Environmental Turbulence - A Strategy to Driving Business Growth in Facing Economic Downturns

Librita Arifiani, Harjanto Prabowo, Asnan Furinto and Wibowo Kosasih

Abstract

Society 5.0 focuses on people and changes from innovation to technological transformation through industrial automation 4.0. In this study, environmental turbulence refers to exogenous factors that give rise to an uncertain and volatile situation that impacts performance. This study was measured by asking respondents' perceptions through explanatory studies and preliminary surveys about market predictability, innovation, and customer preference. Disruptive innovation and environmental turbulence are key creative drivers for reengineering businesses; however, only agile innovation can take advantage of the economic downturn. Exploratory case studies and literature reviews are using to test the antecedent of environmental turbulence, Distinctive Innovation Capabilities, through an innovative business model to firm performance. From a managerial perspective, this study provides a comprehensive view of environmental turbulence's impact, how to develop a DIC strategy for developing an organization's business model, how to achieve it, what variables contribute, and how to relate it to performance. This research's authenticity lies in how management comes up with a practically oriented framework of how organizations shape to be innovative and competitive by constructing common business models. However, this study has limitations due to its qualitative nature and conceptual framework, which needs to be investigated further through large-scale surveys by quantitative research.

Keywords: environment turbulence, firm performance, business model innovation, distinctive innovation capability, Society 5.0

1. Introduction

The modern global economy is on the brink of a new industrial revolution, as evidenced by many actual trends, following the provisions of modern economic theory (economic cycle theory, crisis theory, innovation theory). Overcome the global crisis, a new wave of innovation has needed where Industry 4.0 will become a new global industrial landmark and standard of development in the real economic sector of the entire global economic system [1]. In line with the goals of society 5.0, Industry 4.0 revolutionizes the production industry by increasing operational efficiency, new business models, services, and products. Society 5.0 focuses on using technology developed by Industry 4.0 to benefit humankind by utilizing advanced technology to solve problems and the economy. This study identifies that disruption of innovation through environmental turbulence offers opportunities to drive business development. Society 5.0 focuses on people and changes from innovation to technological transformation through industrial automation 4.0 [2, 3]. In this study, environmental turbulence refers to exogenous factors that give rise to uncertain and volatile situations that impact business performance [4, 5].

While some companies view environmental instability as a risk that threatens performance, it has understood as a threat and an opportunity for more entrepreneurial firms. It opens opportunities for the growth of various new businesses accompanied by increasingly fierce competition [6]. The desire to find ways to overcome turbulence and create growth and success from turbulence drives companies to think and act. Rapid technological advances have led to significant business developments and changes [7]. Likewise, as reported by The Global Competitiveness Report 2017–2018, the interruption and disruption of technological change create extraordinary possibilities and challenges which strengthen by using the convergence of digital, physical and organic technology that has characterized the rise of the Fourth Industrial Revolution [8].

Environmental turbulence can occur in several factors: technology turbulence, competition intensity, market turbulence, and regulation. The biggest factor is due largely to rapid technological changes and the high intensity of competition marked by customer composition changes, behavior, and preferences. In Indonesia, over the top service (OTT) penetration was long before Covid-19 eroded revenue providers [9, 10]. Even though the operator is experiencing growth, the Telco industry requires a large investment, but the income is low. Although growing, digital services have not replaced declining operator revenues [11, 12]. When environmental turbulence occurs, it causes a direct disruption to company performance. Thus, the company's initial response must be fast to reduce accumulated losses. In the firm's predetermined response model, management reactions are initiated without delay on the rational trigger point, as illustrated in **Figure 1** [13]. Due to the environment's

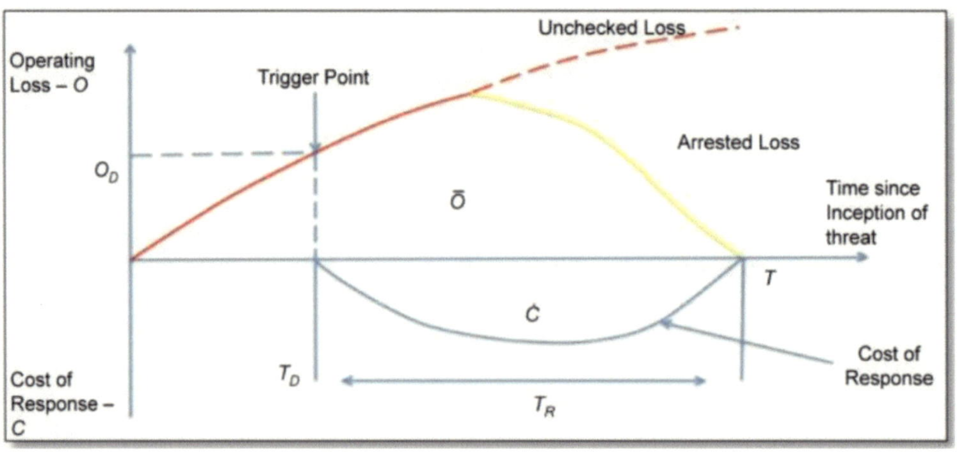

Figure 1.
Decisive model of firm response to a crisis event.

turbulent characteristics, both the base model and the Determinant model of responses are triggered after the event has occurred.

2. Methodology and research gap

In this study, the methodology used is a qualitative systematic literature review on various aspects of the topics discussed, including strategy, distinctive capability, environmental turbulence, and business model strategies. The basic ideas on carrying out such a systematic review had borrowed from leading scholars in the field [14]. Both integrative and interpretive techniques had used to uncover new insights into strategy. Various studies on dynamic strategies and volatile business environments have collected it from various primary qualitative studies conducted using this methodology. Several in-depth studies of the subject matter have carried it out so that conclusions have drawn it. Thus, the literature review's qualitative synthesis has used it as the basis for the arguments discussed in this chapter.

This study is also measured by asking respondents' perceptions through explanatory studies and preliminary surveys on market predictability, innovation, and customer preferences. Disruptive innovation through environmental turbulence is a major creative driver for reengineering businesses. It is not just innovation but *agile innovation* that can take advantage of economic downturns by developing new creative business models by *making new paradigm shifts* [15, 16]. As globalization and digitization evolve, organizations must respond quickly to changing market demands. According to Milan Krstic, 2018 agile innovation is a collaborative process that connects innovation, people, technology, projects, and outputs that impact paradigm shifts driven by competition in the market and rapid technological advances [16]. Agile innovation emphasizes creative and adaptable teamwork in solving complex problems; Lean development focuses on eliminating all losses continuously so that the innovation process is significantly faster [15]. Thus, the company can be fast responding to Changes in Environmental Turbulence to encourage business growth in the face of deteriorating company performance.

Exploratory case studies and literature reviews are using to test environmental turbulence's antecedents, Distinctive Innovation Capabilities, through business model innovation strategies to firm performance [17, 18].

This study fills the gap from the previous study. Since 2000, most business models have focused on organizations' mediating role to mediate technology capabilities and firm performance. Only a handful of research publications so far have examined how organizations innovating should have structured collaborations and interact fluidly [19, 20]. There are no studies that elaborate on how organizations exploit internal resources and structures and how to access, configure, and utilize external resources embedded in business model strategies to produce the ability to manage business turbulence in the industrial evolution of the 4.0 era through Distinctive Innovation Capabilities [21, 22]. This research's authenticity lies in how management produces a practically oriented framework of how organizations shape to be innovative and competitive by building a common business model. However, this study has limitations due to its qualitative nature and conceptual framework, which needs further investigation through large-scale surveys by quantitative research. The conceptualization and investigation of the independent and combined effects of business model innovation, environmental turbulence, and Distinctive Innovation Capabilities structures on organizational agility highlight the importance of complementarity between antecedents and add to the cumulative pool of knowledge in this research area.

From a managerial perspective, this study provides a comprehensive view of environmental turbulence impact, how to develop a Distinctive Innovation Capability strategy for developing an organization's business model, how to achieve it, what variables contribute, and how to relate it to performance. Institutional cooperation requires collaboration in an innovation environment where consumers, companies, universities, and public authorities work together to produce innovation (Quadruple Helix). It means that the resulting research can apply to national development, and higher education is responsive to industrial, customer and social needs [23, 24].

3. Conceptual development

3.1 Environmental turbulence on business model strategy

Companies are operating in a more dynamic environment that affects environmental turbulence that occurs influence business model transformation and business performance. Many studies confirm that several conditions in the Study of Environmental Turbulence and Model Transformation & Business Models affect company performance [25–28]. The more turbulent an environment, companies must rely on innovation to neutralize the outdated threats of products and technology and take advantage of new technological opportunities to create new business models that can support company performance [29, 30]. However, according to [31] pragmatically, some problems will be missed and become strategic surprises even at the most sophisticated environmental scanning method. The recent economic downturn and current pressures on the market have increased the need for leaders to have a strategic business model plan [32]. Organizations whose historical business models have based on organic growth must now strategically position themselves taking into account the new 'rules of the game' and develop a posture that increases strategic, managerial aggressiveness [33].

The process of forming a volatile environment is inseparable from the influence of technology, the emergence of a new economic order, changing values and lifestyles, and the availability of an exchange of information flows, goods and services with a decreasing price trend accompanied by the high speed of the flow of goods/services and the dissemination of information. The emergence of an economic model of sharing transportation and accommodation has disrupted business establishment. Several studies have confirmed the relationship between environmental turbulence and business strategy models and then show that it successfully competitive advantage. Besides, it mediates the role of business model innovation to show that there is a relationship, and the results of several studies suggest that business model innovation has a positive effect on company performance [34, 35].

The description above means the higher the organization's ability to provide the right solutions with a good business model innovation strategy that can provide added value to the organization. Then the innovative business model will perform better in facing competitive advantages in the telecommunications industry. Therefore, it had assumed that environmental turbulence influences business innovation. According to [36], human resources and capabilities are important components of a company's competitive advantage in a resource-based view. The concept of turbulence was initially introduced in 1965 by Emery and Trist. The business environment has been influencing by several components (competition, customers, suppliers, shareholders, public markets, regulatory bodies, legislative bodies, technology, economics, and society) [37]. Environmental turbulence influences the external environment or changes in the future [38, 39]. Based on the contingency

DOI: http://dx.doi.org/10.5772/intechopen.95054

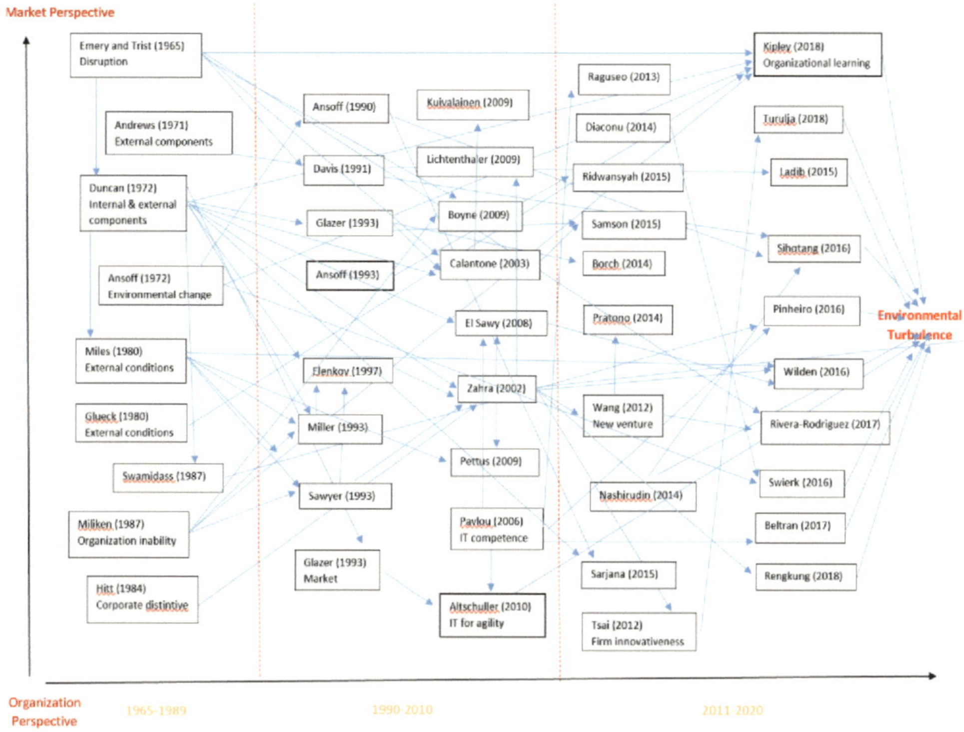

Figure 2.
Theoretical foundation of environmental turbulence. Source: Various publication

theory [40, 41], organizations react to environmental changes, and organizational strategies are determined based on environmental conditions that occur. **Figure 2** shows that many studies on environmental turbulence strategies with a link and difference focus have described it as pedigrees for the theoretical foundation of environmental turbulence from the market and organization perspective.

This study ends with the definition of environmental turbulence for the Telecommunication Industry. Organizational ability to project business planning creatively, flexibly, and adaptively to anticipate potential disruptors, new regulations, technology changes, competition, social patterns, and consumer lifestyles. The dimension of environmental turbulence in this study is; Dynamics - the extent to which the company's environmental components' elements remain the same over time or a continuous flux [42]. The degree of dynamism (instability) has influenced it by changing environmental change and change intensity. Complexity - Increasing number of elements and their interdependence [43], homogeneity/heterogeneity [44] contribute to environmental complexity. Predictability - uncertainty, or ignorance, is a dimension related to the extent of causation and the availability of information about change contributing to the level of uncertainty [39, 45].

3.2 Distinctive innovation capability and firm performance

The literature on strategic management shows different capabilities or competencies as an important part of an organization's resources and competitive advantage. Mintzberg and Quinn [46] argue that Distinctive Innovation capability, as a competitive advantage source, provides the basis for a sustainable competitive advantage [43]. Meanwhile, Drucker [47] and Cavusgil et al. [48] discussed the importance of the ability of innovation for organizations to survive in an unstable environment [46, 47]. Innovation capability had proposed as a high-level integration capability, namely, forming and managing various capabilities [48]. Organizations with this innovation capability can integrate their company's core capabilities and resources to stimulate innovation successfully [49, 50].

According to Amabile [51] and quoted by Zhao et al. [52] states that innovation capability is the application of knowledge relevant to the achievement of value in an organization. Teece and Pisano [53] and Teece et al. [54] suggested that the winners in the global market are companies that demonstrate timely responsiveness and innovation that is fast and flexible [55, 56], together with management's ability to coordinate effectively and re-apply internal and external competencies [57]. However, Miranda and Figueiredo [58] distinguish routine and innovative companies based on technological innovation capabilities with the factors that shape vision and strategy capabilities [51, 52], utilization of competency bases, organizational intelligence, creativity and idea management, organizational structures and systems, culture and climate and technology management [53]. Saunila defines innovation capabilities by influencing an organization's ability to manage innovation [53]. These aspects include participatory leadership culture, ideation, organizational structure, climate, worker welfare, knowledge development, regeneration, external knowledge [54], and individual activity [59].

This study concludes that Distinctive Innovation capability is the company's ability to develop and manage fast and flexible innovation by leveraging technology management's creative capabilities, knowledge development, integrating capabilities, and core company resources to stimulate innovation and provide added value for companies to gain competitive advantage.

3.3 Business model strategy and innovation capability

Any organization interested in competing in a dynamic market must create unique benefits that enable it to gain a competitive advantage over competitors. However, [60] argues that business has become a global and global market, which increasingly encourages an Innovation Business Model because companies must overcome global challenges. The way to outperform competitors is through innovation. Innovation as a strategy involves creating new ideas, processes, and methods to improve current goods and services or bring them into new products and services [37]. Innovation is needed to maintain the existing competitive position and the competitive advantage that has obtained it. Most studies conclude that business model innovation increases competitive advantage and contributes significantly [58, 61]. Previous studies examined cloud and digital computing as disruptive innovations. Building on this reflection, to better understand business model innovation resulting from accepting a cloud benefit model [36, 62].

Technology has changed organizations must realize that a classic business model, such as buying and selling at a premium price, will no longer work [63]. Technological changes provide the necessary context for understanding the transformation of new digital technologies [64–66]. This article will help understand why this new business model's strategy innovation is important and why everyone should understand the most successful business models. Looking at the business model is essential to understanding how to position a company and generate additional revenue [58, 60, 67]. New business models can also help companies become more resilient to market dynamics and diversify business strategy [68, 69]. Successful disruptive business models are often customer focused. Based on the description above, the higher the organization's ability to provide the right solutions with a good business model innovation strategy that can provide sustainable Business Models, Added value to the organization, the high-level innovation will

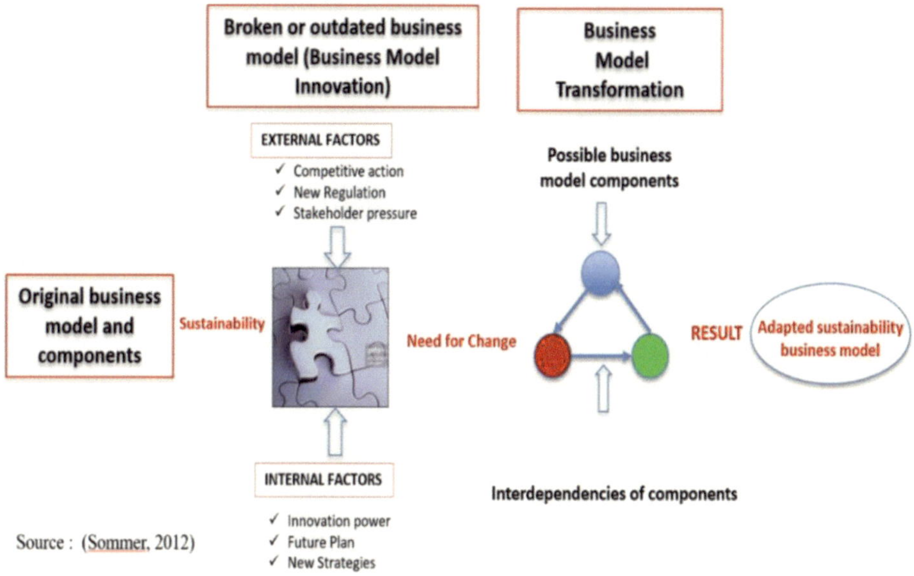

Figure 3.
Sustainability business model transformation.

perform better in the face of competitive advantage [69, 70]. Therefore, a business model paradigm's concept logic can help understand specific innovation to transformation challenges that companies will face when introducing new business models, a simplified schematic overview strategy Sustainability Business Model, reconceptualized from **Figure 3** [71].

4. Development of conceptual framework

An extensive literature review guided the choice of variables for the conceptual framework. Identify the dominant antecedents considered to form the business model innovation strategy and firm performance by developing it through exploratory case studies. Thus, in line with this study, the objectives are to examine the effect of Environmental Turbulence (ET), Distinctive Innovation Ability, and business model innovation influence firm performance (FP). The literature review of the concepts above will answer the questions in this study by explaining how the relationship between Environmental Turbulence (ET), Distinctive Innovation capabilities, and business model innovation affects company performance (FP)?

Therefore, based on the study literature and explanatory case study, this study defined several hypotheses. The following hypotheses have been compiled by modeling the relationships between the variables examined in detail in this section, and a conceptual research model developed, as shown in **Figure 4**.

1. Business model innovation has a positive effect on company performance.

2. Environmental Turbulence (ET) has a positive effect on company performance (FP) directly and indirectly through a business model innovation strategy.

3. Typical Innovation Capabilities have a positive influence on company performance (FP) directly or indirectly through a business model innovation strategy.

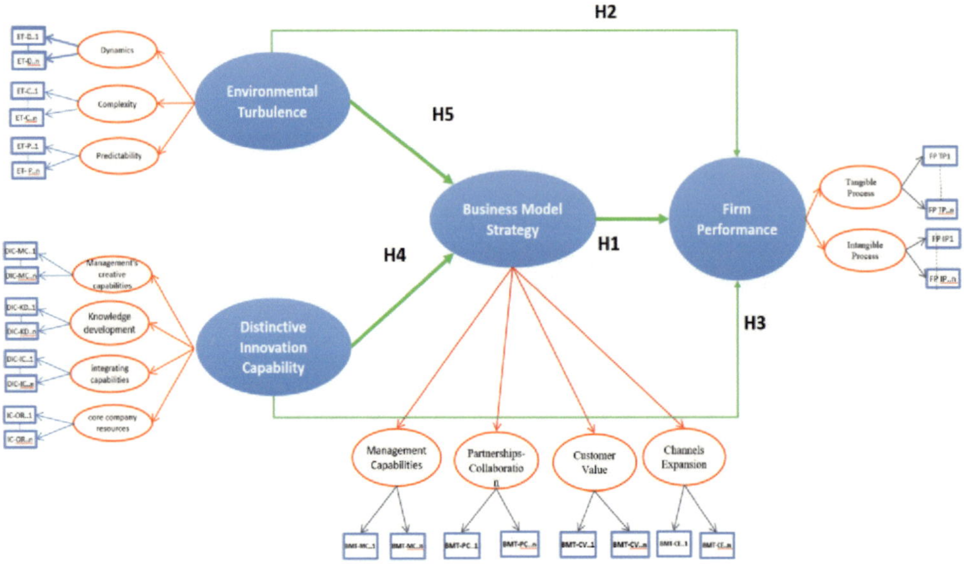

Figure 4.
Conceptual model.

The explanation above and based on the previous literature means that the higher the organization's ability to provide the right solution with a good environmental turbulence strategy that can add value to firm performance, either directly or through an innovation model business strategy. Meanwhile, based on a previous study, the higher its ability to carry out business model innovation and a good distinctive innovation capability, the higher its performance. Therefore, it should have assumed that based on the hypothesis in **Figure 4**, there is an influence between environmental turbulence, business innovation strategy, and distinctive innovation capability on company performance in the telecommunications industry.

5. Conclusion

Exploratory case studies and systematic literature reviews prove that business strategy innovation and firm performance are essential for business success when faced with intense environmental turbulence. Typical Innovation Capabilities and Firm Performance are determined by appropriate revenue in the ongoing market and the expansion of technology and innovation in products for new information for decision-making capabilities [70]. Therefore, innovative portfolio business models are at the center of strategic decision-making capabilities, especially when the complexity of innovation and dynamics increases. This study conceptually develops a framework that connects environmental turbulence, distinctive innovation capabilities, business model innovation, and tests its effect on company performance. This study uses information processing theory to propose and test the antecedents and consequences of a business model innovation strategy.

Innovative business model capabilities are a continuous change from new business strategies to keep pace with market developments, competitive advantage, and performance. Therefore, innovation capabilities are not simply the ability to successfully run a new business or manage mainstream capabilities. However, innovation capability is about synthesizing three paradigms, enabling innovative companies to produce new products and services that are quality-focused, efficient, and responsive.

This study proposes the idea of a Typical Innovation capability. We have used the innovation management literature and several case studies as examples of Cisco Systems to demonstrate how innovation capabilities synthesize new and mainstream flows to achieve effective innovation performance. The next section identifies the elements of makeup innovation capability. Therefore, the innovation capability model aims to build a theoretical framework that highlights the actions managers can take to influence innovation success. However, several attempts have made it use a dynamic capabilities approach to produce a holistic innovation capability model. Organizations focus on innovation and innovation output as a competitive strategy.

Besides, this study has been able to fill the gaps and enhance previous studies on business model innovation strategies. It has explained that the distinctive Innovation capabilities by utilizing the external organizational structure's capabilities and flexibility can face business turbulence. It allows organizations to achieve an increase in business strategy innovation capabilities, high-quality company performance in the face of economic decline, and at the same time, add to this cumulative knowledge study. Investigations of a set of antecedents of distinctive Innovation capabilities, business model innovation strategies, and environmental turbulence on company performance have highlighted the importance of complementarity as critical factors developed in future research.

6. Future research

This research has limitations in telecommunications information, communication, and technology in Indonesia. As an antecedent of the Service Innovation has identified it, and its relationship has presented, large-scale quantitative surveys will test the conceptual framework and further explore each variable's role. Furthermore, future research expands to consider the international implications of research and the broader scope.

7. Management implications/social impact

From a managerial perspective, this research gives organization management a comprehensive view of enhancing innovation business model strategy and consecutively providing a solution to customers and influencing it and their relationships. This study will benefit the telecommunications companies that want to move to digital transformation, which is still an expensive and lengthy process, by using strengthening integrative capability to perfecting internal monetization, but especially overcoming external monetization from the opportunity of environmental turbulence to leap forward. Portfolio managers have suggested it intensify the information system's use as it positively impacts an organization's innovation business performance by intensifying information exchange with internal and external stakeholders.

From the social impact perspective, with the sustainable growth of technology-based companies, through innovative business models, Distinctive Innovation capability and environmental turbulence capabilities, companies can provide general benefits from the microeconomic side to customers and at a macro level to the performance of the company and industry in general. Thus, it can be a driving force for the advancement of digitalized technology knowledge and adopted by the community to prepare development towards society 5.0.

Author details

Librita Arifiani*, Harjanto Prabowo, Asnan Furinto and Wibowo Kosasih
Binus Business School, Bina Nusantara University, Indonesia

*Address all correspondence to: librita.arifiani@binus.ac.id

References

[1] S. K. Rao and R. Prasad, "Impact of 5G Technologies on Industry 4.0," Wirel. Pers. Commun., vol. 100, no. 1, pp. 145-159, 2018.

[2] T. Drolc, "Society 5.0: the shift from technology first to human first," Jul-2020. [Online]. Available: http://www.sloveniatimes.com/society-5-0-the-shift-from-technology-first-to-human-first.

[3] Keidanren, "Toward realization of the new economy and society," *Policy & Action*, vol. 2016. Japan Business Federation, pp. 1-25, 2016.

[4] M. Hamsal and I. G. N. Agung, "Paradoxical strategies and firm performance: The case of Indonesian banking Industry," South East Asian J. Manag., vol. 1, No.1, pp. 43-64, 2007.

[5] J. Sihotang, D. Kartini, and P. Rufaidah, "Environmental Turbulence , Entrepreneurial Orientation and Business Unit Performance : Effects on Dynamic Capabilitie and Strategic Alliance Formation and Its Role To Build Sustainable Competitive Advantage," *Int. J. Econ. Commer. Manag.*, vol. IV, no. 6, pp. 317-351, 2016.

[6] McKinsey, "How disruptive technologies are opening up innovative opportunities in services," 2018.

[7] R. Baumgartner and R. Rauter, "Strategic perspectives of corporate sustainability management to develop a sustainable organization," *J. Clean. Prod.*, vol. 140, no. June 2016, pp. 81-92, 2017.

[8] K. Schwab, "The Global Competitiveness Report 2017-2018," 2017.

[9] Statista, "Indonesia: internet penetration rate 2023," https://www.statista.com/statistics/254460/internet-penetration-rate-in-indonesia/, 2020.

[10] Bisnis.com, "Wabah Corona, Industri Telekomunikasi Minta Insentif," 2020. [Online]. Available: https://teknologi.bisnis.com/read/20200324/101/1217660/wabah-corona-industri-telekomunikasi-minta-insentif. [Accessed: 22-Jun-2020].

[11] J. Plate and Ismail, "Industry Summit, Promoting Digital Indonesia," 2020. .

[12] F. Vendrell-Herrero, O. F. Bustinza, G. Parry, and N. Georgantzis, "Servitization, digitization and supply chain interdependency," Ind. Mark. Manag., vol. 60, pp. 69-81, 2017.

[13] D. Kipley, A. Lewis, and R. Jewe, "Entropy - Disrupting Ansoff's five levels of environmental turbulence," Bus. Strateg. Ser., vol. 13, no. 6, pp. 251-262, 2012.

[14] R. P. Gephart, "Qualitative Research and the Academy of Management Journal," Acad. Manag. J., vol. 47, no. 4, pp. 454-462, Aug. 2004.

[15] B. Vine, V. Guggisberg, and A. Back, "Agile Innovation for Next Generation Mobile Business," *Stud. Corpus-Based Socioling.*, no. December, pp. 197-218, 2017.

[16] M. Krstić, A. Skorup, and G. Lapčević, "Trends in agile innovation management," *Int. Rev.*, no. 3-4, pp. 58-70, 2018.

[17] J. J. Kranz, A. Hanelt, and L. M. Kolbe, "Understanding the influence of absorptive capacity and ambidexterity on the process of business model change – the case of on-premise and cloud-computing software," Inf. Syst. J., vol. 26, no. 5, pp. 477-517, 2016.

[18] R. Blundel, "The co-evolution of technological capabilities and industrial dynamics in competing innovation

networks," Ind. Innov., vol. 13, no. 3, pp. 313-334, 2006.

[19] D. J. Teece, "Fundamental Issues in Strategy: Time to Reassess?," Strateg. Manag. Rev., vol. 1, no. 1, pp. 103-144, 2020.

[20] S. A. Cavalcante, "Understanding the impact of technology on firms' business models," Eur. J. Innov. Manag., vol. 16, no. 3, pp. 285-300, 2013.

[21] V. Story, L. O'Malley, and S. Hart, "Roles, role performance, and radical innovation competences," Ind. Mark. Manag., vol. 40, no. 6, pp. 952-966, 2011.

[22] C. C. J. Cheng, J. S. Chen, C. C. J. Cheng, and J. Chen, "Breakthrough innovation : the roles of dynamic innovation capabilities and open innovation activities," 2014.

[23] R. Arnkil and A. Järvensivu, "Exploring the Quadruple Helix," 2010.

[24] Bappenas, "Visi Indonesia 2045," *Visi Indones. 2045*, vol. 1, no. September, p. 48, 2017.

[25] L. Kester, E. J. Hultink, and A. Griffin, "An empirical investigation of the antecedents and outcomes of NPD portfolio success," J. Prod. Innov. Manag., vol. 31, no. 6, pp. 1199-1213, 2014.

[26] M. Porter, *Four Competitive Strategies*. 1991.

[27] O. J. Borch and B. M. Batalden, "Business-process management in high-turbulence environments: the case of the offshore service vessel industry," Marit. Policy Manag., vol. 42, no. 5, pp. 481-498, 2015.

[28] F. Ridwansyah, R. Oktaviani, and I. T. Saptono, "Fit Analysis of Indosat Dompetku Business Model Using a Strategic Diagnosis Approach," Indones. J. Bus. Entrep., vol. 1, no. 3, pp. 137-147, 2015.

[29] H.-A. Rivera-Rodríguez, T. Garcia-Merino, and V. Santos-Alvarez, "How to Thrive in Turbulent Business Environments: Case Colombia's Mobile Telephony Industry," Mediterr. J. Soc. Sci., vol. 8, no. 3, pp. 133-141, 2017.

[30] T. Clauss, M. Abebe, C. Tangpong, and M. Hock, "Strategic Agility, Business Model Innovation, and Firm Performance: An Empirical Investigation," *IEEE Trans. Eng. Manag.*, vol. PP, pp. 1-18, 2019.

[31] M. Carver and D. Kipley, "Ansoff's Strategic Issue Management System: A Validation for Use in the Banking Industry during High Turbulent Environments," *Bus. Renaiss. Q.*, vol. 5, no. 2, p. 59, 2010.

[32] M. Abbas and M. Ul Hassan, "Moderating impact of environmental turbulence on business innovation and business performance," Pakistan J. Commer. Soc. Sci., vol. 11, no. 2, pp. 576-596, 2017.

[33] J. Frishammar and V. Parida, "Circular Business Model Transformation: A roadmap for Incumbent Firms," Calif. Manage. Rev., pp. 1-25, 2018.

[34] G. Farkas, "The Effects of Strategic Orientations and Perceived Environment on Firm Performance," J. Compet., vol. 8, no. 1, pp. 55-65, 2016.

[35] S. Denning and Stephen, "How to make the whole organization Agile," Strateg. Leadersh., vol. 43, no. 6, pp. 10-17, Nov. 2015.

[36] D. Brooke, "The Relationship Between An Innovation Orientation And Competitive Strategy," Int. J. Innov. Manag., vol. 14, no. 02, pp. 331-357, Apr. 2010.

[37] K. Zalewska-kurek, S. Kandemir, B. G. Englis, and P. D. Englis, "Development of Market-Driven Business Models in the IT Industry . How Firms Experiment with Their Business Models?," J. Bus. Model., vol. 4, no. 3, pp. 48-67, 2016.

[38] Tomczak, *Market-oriented Business Unit Planning*. 2018.

[39] N. Azad and M. Rikhtegar, "An exploration study on building market oriented business," Manag. Sci. Lett., vol. 3, pp. 1403-1408, 2013.

[40] L. Donaldson, "The Contingency Theory of Organizations," Found. Organ. Sci., vol. 3, no. 2, pp. 1-345, 2001.

[41] M. Nekhili, H. Chakroun, and T. Chtioui, "Women's Leadership and Firm Performance: Family Versus Nonfamily Firms," J. Bus. Ethics, vol. 153, no. 2, pp. 291-316, 2018.

[42] R. B. Duncan, "Characteristics of organizational environments and perceived environmental uncertainty," *Adm Sci Q*, vol. 17, no. 3, pp. 313-327; 313, 1972.

[43] H. Mintzberg, B. Ahlstrand, and J. Lampel, *Strategy Safari A Guided Tourthrough The Wilds Of Strategic Management*. 1998.

[44] K. G. Smith, W. Ferrier, and H. Ndofor, "Competitive Dynamics Research: Critique and Future Directions," in *The Blackwell Handbook ofStrategic Management,* and J. S. H. A. Hitt , R. Edward Freeman, Ed. Blackwell Publishing Ltd., 2006, pp. 315-361.

[45] R. BERGER, "How to survive in the VUCA world," 2018. [Online]. Available: https://studylib.net/doc/8319838/how-to-survive-in-the-vuca-world. [Accessed: 19-Jun-2019].

[46] S. Jha, "Management Philosophy of Peter F . Drucker : A Critique," Apeejay Bus. Rev., vol. 10, no. 1, pp. 54-61, 2009.

[47] S. H. Seggie, D. Kim, and S. T. Cavusgil, "Do supply chain IT alignment and supply chain interfirm system integration impact upon brand equity and firm performance?," J. Bus. Res., vol. 59, no. 8, pp. 887-895, 2006.

[48] L. Sugandi, "Dampak Implementasi Change Management Pada Organisasi," ComTech, vol. 4, no. 9, pp. 313-323, 2013.

[49] V. Nilakant, "Change Management: Altering Mindsets in A Global Context - V Nilakant, S Ramnarayan - Google Buku," 2006. [Online]. Available: https://books.google.co.id/books?id=ibfBTKs8_-cC&pg=PA57&lpg=PA57&dq=Distinctive+Capabilities,change+management&source=bl&ots=QIHDuIKO1-&sig=h_zUPEkOwEuGhXAvvfVzKXD83qY&hl=id&sa=X&ved=0ahUKEwiRzvvj9draAhUPMt8KHbXuAW04FBDoAQg5MAI#v=onepage&q=Distinctive . [Accessed: 28-Apr-2018].

[50] M. T. Bolívar-Ramos and V. García, "Technological distinctive competencies and organizational learning: Effects on organizational innovation to improve firm performance," J. Eng. Technol. Manag. - JET-M, vol. 29, no. 3, pp. 331-337, Jul. 2012.

[51] A. Roseno, D.- Frederiksberg, and Z. Universität, "Distinctive dynamic capabilities for new business creation : sensing , seizing , scaling and separating Ellen Enkel and Florian Mezger," vol. 8, no. 2, pp. 197-234, 2013.

[52] C. Romero, "Administrative Sciences Distinctive Innovation Capabilities of Argentine Software Companies with High Innovation Results and Impacts," 2018.

[53] L. Achtenhagen, L. Melin, and L. Naldi, "Dynamics of business models - strategizing, critical capabilities and activities for sustained value creation," Long Range Plann., vol. 46, no. 6, pp. 427-442, 2013.

[54] D. Palacios, Æ. I. Gil, and Æ. F. Garrigos, "The impact of knowledge management on innovation and entrepreneurship in the biotechnology and telecommunications industries," pp. 291-301, 2009.

[55] C. P. Killen, "Managing portfolio interdependencies: The effects of visual data representations on project portfolio decision making," Int. J. Manag. Proj. Bus., vol. 10, no. 4, pp. 856-879, 2017.

[56] D. Jonas, "Empowering project portfolio managers: How management involvement impacts project portfolio management performance," Int. J. Proj. Manag., vol. 28, no. 8, pp. 818-831, 2010.

[57] D. J. Teece, "Explicating dynamic capabilities: the nature and micro foundations of (sustainable) enterprise performance," Strateg. Manag. J., vol. 28, no. 13, pp. 1319-1350, Dec. 2007.

[58] T. M. Kising'u, P. G. S. Namusonge, and D. F. M. Mwirigi, "The Role of Organizational Innovation in Sustainable Competitive Advantage in Universities in Kenya," Int. J. Soc. Sci. Humanit. Invent., vol. 3, no. 9, pp. 2762-2786, 2016.

[59] J. M. Pinheiro, M. T. Preto, L. F. Lages, and G. M. Silva, "Knowledge creation, turbulence, and manufacturing flexibility roles in business performance and operations performance," *Knowl. Manag.*, no. 1996, pp. 16-28, 2016.

[60] S. K. Rao and R. Prasad, "Telecom Operators' Business Model Innovation in a 5G World," J. Multi Bus. Model Innov. Technol., vol. 4, no. 3, pp. 149-178, 2018.

[61] B. Wooldridge and S. W. Floyd, "The Strategy Process , Middle Management Involvement , and Organizational Performance," vol. 11, no. 3, pp. 231-241, 2016.

[62] B. E. Marchiori, C. E. Carraher, and K. Stiles, "Journal of Technology Management in China Company Article Title Page," J. Technol. Manag. China2, vol. 9, no. 3, pp. 274-288, 2014.

[63] H. Kagermann, "Change Through Digitization—Value Creation in the Age of Industry 4.0," in *Management of Permanent Change*, Wiesbaden: Springer Fachmedien Wiesbaden, 2015, pp. 23-45.

[64] A. Osterwalder and Y. Pigneur, *Business Model Generation: A Handbook for Visionaries, Game Changers, and Challengers*, vol. 5, no. 7. 2010.

[65] M. Mikusz, T. Schafer, T. Taraba, and C. Jud, "Transforming the connected car into a business model innovation," *Proc. - 2017 IEEE 19th Conf. Bus. Informatics, CBI 2017*, vol. 1, pp. 247-256, 2017.

[66] C. Arnold, D. Kiel, and K.-I. Voigt, "Innovative Business Models for the Industrial Internet of Things," *BHM Berg- und Hüttenmännische Monatshefte*, 2017.

[67] M. P. W, "Relationship Between Innovation Strategies and Competitive Advantage in the Logistics Firms in Mombasa County , Kenya By Mburu Paul Wanyoike a Research Project Submitted in Partial Fulfillment of the Requirements for the Award of the Degree of Master of B," 2016.

[68] A. A. Gaivoronski, P. J. Nesse, and O. B. Erdal, "Internet service provision and content services: Paid peering and competition between internet providers," Econ. Res. Electron. Netw., vol. 18, no. 1, pp. 43-79, 2017.

[69] R. R. Nelson and S. G. Winter, *An evolutionary theory of economic change*, vol. 93, no. 2. 1982.

[70] El-Darwiche Bahjat and Rupp Christine, "Aspiring to digital simplicity and clarity in strategic identity," 2017.

[71] A. Sommer, *Sustainable Production, Life Cycle Engineering and Management (Managing Green Business Model Transformations)*. 2012.

Chapter 7

COVID-19: Turning a Threat into an Opportunity for the Circular Economy

Jean Pierre Doussoulin

Abstract

The current crisis dominates everything from health to day-to-day life. But it will pass over within a relatively short space of time and the economic recession seems likely to reverse the long-standing pattern. Given the gravity of the circumstances, nations have been constrained to undertake unusual approach arrangements. This article proposes a framework of the COVID-19 effect following analysis and comparison of the most prominent concepts of the public health and circular economy. Our paper helps to identify the positions of each of these concepts with regard to public health, environmental sustainability and economic growth. This study enriches the literature on the environmental sciences and public health by providing analysis of the effects of the policies. Finally, this article recognizes that there must be local action priorities that allow for small and sequential wins in economic, health and environmental aspects in the territory.

Keywords: COVID-19, circular economy, waste, health, growth, environment

1. Introduction

As a result of this pandemic, we can note the disappearance of questions and conversations related to climate change [1]. It seems that the lack of progress towards the objectives of the Paris agreement has disappeared into the background. What would once have been the center of attention in most forums and agendas does not even reach the inside pages of magazines or newscasts. Our global consciousness has shifted towards survival and transcendence, as a species, which are immediate threats to our lives [2].

This desire for transcendence allows us to analyze what happens when we are closer to the top of the pyramid and all our basic concepts are covered as in Maslow's pyramid [3]. With the pandemic around the world, we have all been taken down on some levels and we are now looking to protect ourselves and our loved ones.

On the surface, it seems that all efforts, all activities and all initiatives have shifted away from the greatest threat to our planet, climate change, towards the immediate and more tangible threat to our lives of COVID-19 [4].

The desire for transcendence can also be expressed towards transhumanism and environmental sustainability. Transhumanism is a social movement predicated on the belief that we can and should leave behind our biological condition by merging with technology [5]. Environmental sustainability is responsibly interacting with the planet to maintain natural resources and give the ability of future generations to meet their needs. It can be interpreted as an steady state economy [6]. This status depends on legal, thermodynamic, and economic aspects of ecosystem services [7, 8].

This chapter proposes a new regard of the circular economy following analysis of the most prominent issues related with COVID-19, government responses to the crisis and sustainability.

The significance of this article is that it addresses the criticisms of the circular economy paradigms by considering three dimensions of analysis related to the COVID-19 outbreak [9]. The increased demand for sustainable production processes post COVID-19 justifies the need for more effective policies with a focus on human health [1, 10].

2. Methodology

The methodology used in this paper takes sustainability, health care, economic growth and dimensions to provide an analysis related to COVID-19. **Figure 1** presents the analysis of how these three dimensions might be reinterpreted using the framework proposed by Doussoulin [9]. As shown in **Figure 1**, when π = 100%, z = 0 and w = 0, all attention dedicated by the government are apportioned to economic growth. Alternatively, if π = 0, z = 0 and w = 100%, then all attention is given to health care. It is also possible the attention to the earth as a natural resource, this can be represented by the point where π =0, z = 100% and w = 0, which corresponds to a sustainable future [11–13].

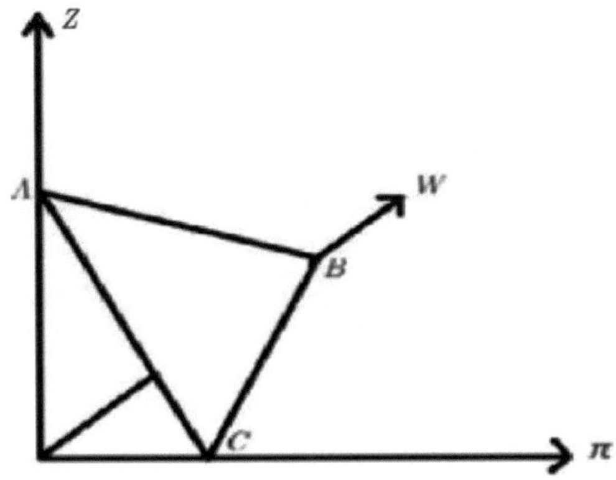

Figure 1.
Three dimensions: Economic growth, health care and sustainability. Source: [9]

3. Discussion

This section outlines a set of matters involving the COVID-19 crisis through the exploration of three dimensions: sustainability, health care and economic growth, as follow:

3.1 Sustainability

3.1.1 Industrial circular economy

The circular economy has rapidly gathered momentum within sustainable development initiatives due to its potential for decoupling economic development and growth from resource consumption [14, 15]. The industrial circular economy corresponds to $\pi = 0$, $z = 100\%$ and $w = 0$ in **Figure 1**. Manufacturing companies play a critical role in the implementation of the circular economy at the industrial level. Success with this role requires a rethinking of the overall value generation logic and the redefinition of business success, by reconfiguring existing business models or creating new business models for the circular economy [16, 17].

The transition of manufacturing companies' business models to the circular economy is still limited, with low market penetration across sectors. Among several external and internal barriers, manufacturing companies face shortcomings in capabilities and skills and require knowledge and scientific-based guidance for business modeling within the context of the circular economy [18, 19].

Academic literature is unable to support companies adequately, due to a core gap related to the lack of systematized practices to provide guidance and advice to manufacturing companies during the design of business models for the circular economy [20]. Based on this gap, a design research methodology was applied in this research, with the objective of developing a theoretical framework to provide guidance and advice for policy-makers and stakeholders [21].

3.1.2 Pressure on the MSW industry

The workload of the MSW (management solid waste) industry has increased due to significant rises in household consumption in Japan [22] and the construction sector in France [23].

The Center for Disease Control (CDC) is saying the same as the World Health Organization and also what Ocean is saying, that solid waste is not an effective vector for the transmission of corona virus from one person to another by being within six feet of that person. Something people need to be aware of when they are at work, whether it is collecting trash, recycling material or a disposal facility. The CDC just late last week, issued a new waste specific fact sheet [24].

That indicated that corona virus can live on cardboard for up to 24 hours, which causes some concerns in our industry. People are also urged to delay their spring cleaning. Individuals will admit that this has not always been succesfully communicated [25]. As people at home with a lot spare time, they are using it to clean out their attics, garages and basements, and this is generating a significant amount of material that has stressed the system to some extent. Authors are also communicating the importance of not reusing gloves and masks that people are now wearing and that they should be thrown in the trash after use [26].

We can agree that generally individuals do not want to recycle. The material, even though it is mostly made of plastic, is not recycled on the curbside and unfortunately, what we have seen a great deal is many people throwing away gloves and masks on the street, in parking lots and in parks which is bad for public health in the environment [27]. The fact that some facilities are closing due to small amounts of coronavirus on things that are being handled, at a time when the commodity pricing is actually going up, is ironic. There have been a number of facilities that perform recycling that have actually closed. They closed because they were unable to provide sufficient social distancing between workers. However most facilities have been either installing Plexiglas separators between the sorters or pickers on the line or they have been separating the pickers [28, 29].

The commercial sector in the United States shut down a major source of recovered paper. A major source of clean, recovered paper was lost, and so it is our hope that, as the United States returns to something like the new normal, we will see that those paper sources in the commercial sector will be available to recycling facilities [30].

There is an interaction at the weighing facilities and to reduce the potential of exposure to the attendants who work there, the use of cash and the signing of documents is being eliminated. Other steps are being taken to ensure there is as little interaction as possible with customers at drop-off centers, where people go to drop off various types of materials such as glass, books or batteries. Those facilities have seen a significant increase in the number of customers that they are receiving so there is a need to keep the customers six feet apart from each other and also from the staff. Disposal facilities also pose a number of hazards and challenges when a waste, hauler or a private citizen goes through a small facility, whether it is by dumper truck or to bring some boxes from the household, hazardous waste or other material [31].

These facilities are urging people to wear masks. Some people are not happy being asked to wear them at some of the facilities. Some facilities have higher safety measures to maintain distance and enforce their rules. Curbside recycling collection has been suspended in several communities [31]. For the use of vehicles, at recycling plants and composting plants, a number of issues in handling the materials and during maintenance were coming up. In the United States, the drop-off centers are adding to the burden. People are very slowly beginning to go back to work and it is our expectation that this is going to continue and some authors will argue a decrease in the amount of residential waste and an increase in the amount of commercial waste being generated [32].

Things were coming to a point where waste management was at risk of stopping because of the worries of the workers and some of their employees, basically there was a very short time frame to sort this out. If it is a commercial collection, maybe it could be stopped, if it is a household collection, it probably could not be, and it cannot be run by a single person because of health and safety or other issues. People could then think about transporting individuals separately through the collection point, and some local authorities in the UK have been taking that approach where they have individually taken collections, from the curbside where the transfer has been done. Other solutions might be screens in the cabs, therefore there is a guidance on screens [33].

There are health and safety issues in assessing the safety of the screen and the material. Whether or not the driver can see through it, whether they can get out of a vehicle safely if there is an accident, and if it is effective in case somebody sneezes and if it will really stop an aerosol from circulating in a cab. There has been quite a lot in the media about viral load and long term exposure to viral load [34].

To what extent can some of the lessons learned in UK composting sites and reducing work exposure to aerosols be translated to the virus or are the particles too small? Authors argued that the reason that has happened is because people in their homes are seeing all this waste being generated and being putting out on the curb which is not usual and seeing it taken away by trucks [35]. Normally, when the garbage truck comes to the house, people are not at home, they are at work, and so the fact that there are these people out there every single day performing this essential service when citizens are told to stay at home has been a way to reinforce the importance of the industry. Authors argue that in the long term, this will benefit the industry in a number of things, but in the short-term, we will continue to have challenges related to reducing exposure because, unfortunately, the virus is very contagious compared to other diseases. It spreads easily, and at least some component of the virus can live on cardboard for a while [36].

3.1.3 Facilities dedicated to hazardous waste treatment

There is limited research on the viability of this virus in the recycling stream. As pointed out earlier, we need to make sure that those workers who are working with recycling are not touching the recycled material and being infected by COVID-19 [37].

It is a terrible pandemic, so in terms of waste we have to make sure that people are managing it safely. It also highlights deficiencies in the system in the past which individuals are now having to correct to ensure the health and safety of the workers properly. Maybe now people need to address how we protect our workers in general. People need to make the point and highlight the fact that the message must be quite clear to the citizens and to the overall community through different channels that separate collection and recycling services are a part of the overall waste management system and part of those essential services that must keep running [38]. It would be a bad thing if the message that was sent out was that these kinds of services can be interrupted or can be stopped. The support of the people is needed and would be difficult to get back if lost, as all international researchers assert [39].

It would be interesting to analyze where facilities dedicated to hazardous waste treatment are lacking and countries where sufficient capacities exist. The import of hazardous waste from outside the EU is worrying not because of the lack of business, but because it means that potentially stockpiles of hazardous waste will grow and grow in the coming months, with all associated risks for health and the environment. Authors argue that increase is not really the right word to best define the situation. It would be better to say shift: there is a shift in terms of the nature of hazardous waste, a shift from non-dedicated to dedicated hazardous waste treatment facilities and a shift in the internal movement of waste [40].

It is possible to improve recycling in the time of COVID-19. Particularly, People have to think about the fact that if houses are separating their recyclables or households, they cannot contaminate themselves. There is no reason that any city should tell its citizens not to continue recycling. The point is that only recyclables from one household, which only people in that household have touched, are put out for collection for recycling or put into a bin where somebody else will empty. It does require that cities who find recycling to be important at the city level should think about extra storage and extra capacity.

3.2 Health care

3.2.1 Personal protective equipment and COVID-19

We are living in unstable and uncertain times due to current health, economic and social instabilities [41]. The significant challenges to the waste industry are putting authorities and waste workers under significant pressure. That is where it is our duty to ensure that our members and the waste management industry have knowledge and information to keep our towns and cities clean and healthy. Proper waste management is an essential public service that cannot be overlooked in this time of crisis [42].

Pandemics prove to the public worldwide that for crucial issues, scientific support of political decisions and data-driven decision-making is absolutely necessary for a proper response so a new relationship between science and policy is needed. This is something that has been lacking in waste management the last ten or fifteen years [43].

This period marks a return of single-use plastics after three years of efforts to ban them under a specific framework. Thus, single-use plastics are coming back today and this time also with gloves, with masks and with personal protective equipment that might be infectious [27].

This difficult period is not a reason to change our policies and circular economics for plastics and single-use plastics. Authors argue that the plastic industry is trying to use the pandemics as an excuse to delay any new regulation or secretly use plastics, both at a European or national level [44, 45].

We have a range of wastes being generated at the moment and initially it comes down to segregation and while people may be seeing the volumes of personal protective equipment (PPE) and other medical wastes increasing, we have to look at the relative risk of those wastes. Waste from people who treat a COVID-19 patient, will be particularly risky. [46].

A lot of medical waste will be produced. There will also be some pharmaceutical waste. There will be ventilated type waste; there will be collection mechanisms for contaminated waste, and proper, genuine medical waste. These wastes need to be collected and treated appropriately, not necessarily by incineration where alternative treatments are in place. They should be genuinely treated as infectious medical wastes. There will be a lot more medical waste in our general waste. It has been argued that if we start to call them social distancing wastes rather than medical wastes, even though they look like medical wastes, some distinctions may be able to be made [47, 48].

3.2.2 COVID-19 and HIV virus

Authors claim that many of the patients who have COVID-19 who are very sick and also have other conditions as well. In addition to dealing with the pandemic, people also need to consider that those wastes may also have hepatitis or HIV, as well as those other viruses that we would normally manage as healthcare waste [40, 49]. Individuals have to be aware of the fact that, while this is a very serious pandemic, there are other people that are sick with other diseases, and we have to ensure that these other conditions are managed.

As well as waste, there are other contaminants that could be present. People should be treating anything that is known to be infectious or reliably suspected, and this is where it is not necessary that PPE is classified as medical waste. While authors are seeing pressure from an increasing volume and a decrease in weight into the system, we have to still make sure that we are taking care of health. In effect, COVID-19 is like a little ball of genetic material with a fatty inside with a little protein sticking out of it. People need to ensure that people can use heat when necessary, but not necessarily high temperance in washing. It would be useful to have facilities for washing clothes and washing linen. These wastes should be kept out of the waste stream. People need to ensure that the threat against waste workers is mitigated and that may be done by social distancing and PPE. Welfare facilities that ensure that people can wash their hands should also be given because it is not a good idea that more people get sick [50].

It would also be useful to have facilities to ensure that people can maintain not only their personal hygiene, but also environmental hygiene. As authors argue, as there is an increase in the volume of waste arriving to waste facilities, all need to be operating effectively in this situation. It depends on existing infrastructures and the capacities for the treatment of hazardous waste and it also depends on the strictness of lockdown and how it impacts the industrial activities. It is important to say that the other waste treatment facilities never stop during the crisis. Part of the healthcare waste is treated in hazardous waste incinerators and, during this period, where the quantity and mostly the volume of this care waste rises by twenty to forty percent, all permitted capacities are used [31, 51].

A change in the distribution of the different categories of hazardous waste has been observed. Some industrial activities work intensively, for example, the pharmaceutical sector, and others slow down or have even stopped completely, such as the automotive industry and all the suppliers, hazardous waste from households and hazardous waste in small quantities, drums or buckets from refuse collectors. Another important aspect is those non dedicated facilities which treat hazardous waste as a side activity, have slowed down or drastically reduced or even shut down, such as part of the cement industry due to the stopping of activity in the construction sector. Companies have dedicated operators for the treatment of hazardous waste, and they have been able to take over. If we take the case of Europe, we face an increase of transboundary shipments from within the EU to countries where treatment capacities are lacking [38].

3.2.3 Medical waste recycling and government issue

Waste management has been classed as an essential public service in most countries, which means waste management professionals must navigate the health and safety risks related to coronavirus, although, information about the virus is still evolving [52]. It is essential that countries ensure that waste workers, especially frontline collection and processing employees, are afforded maximum protection and remain safe and can support communities in mitigating the spread of the virus [44]. The medical issue corresponds to $\pi = 0$, $z = 0$ and $w = 100\%$ in **Figure 1**.

Some governments have been talking somewhat about the role of the public in protecting solid waste workers [53]. One of the byproducts of the corona virus epidemic has been a very significant increase in the amount of residential recycling and that includes making waste materials safe. The government recommends that people do not use loose tissues or wipes to clean down something that could impact the workers [10].

French and Spanish citizens claim that the first challenge at the beginning of the crisis was to state which of their activities was essential, ensuring that all employees who have to be on-site to operate the facilities can circulate freely during lockdown and be able to secure supplies opportunely. Also, subcontractors facilitate the help of authorities in case of problems. The second action concerned, behaviors and work practices. New safety measures should be applied in order to protect workers by adapting the management of operation teams and their way of working and deploying teleworking. For all others, and last but not least, all necessary personal protective equipment should be provided to everybody, which is probably the trickiest point during this crisis [54, 55].

3.3 Economic growth in COVID-19

We are in the middle of the storm, which does not allow us to see clearly what is coming. But at present the most important thing is to take care of people's health and then employment, which means that people have to understand that we are experiencing a crisis.

A recurring question relates to the time frame in which we will emerge from this crisis. In this sense, the recovery curve represents the impact of coronavirus on the economy. This can have a V- shape if the stoppage is abrupt and the reactivation is rapid, which would not be the effect of COVID-19 for many countries. If economic indicators take longer to reach the levels they were before the recession, a U- shape may appear. Finally, if the crisis implies a recession in the economy and a very slow recovery, we would be describing the L-shape [56].

There is widespread uncertainty about the economic effects of the crisis [57]. Some authors argue that the recovery will be similar to that which occurred in China between 2005 and 2013, following the tendency of L-shaped growth [58]. This economic effect may be very different in the other countries. In this case, what counts is the adaptation of the population to this "new normality" [59].

This means that people have to adapt quickly, and be flexible in how they proceed. People have to understand that spirits are exacerbated, and act accordingly, both for employees and employers [60]. The second thing is to know that we are in a situation that demands priorities, and here it is the health issue. It would be interesting to measure this problem and understand that very complex weeks are coming, and take measures to try to stop or mitigate the impacts on the environment through the application of waste management policies [44].

In the first part of this chapter we described three dimensions of analysis, now we will briefly delve into the economic dimension. The economic growth and labor issues corresponds to $\pi = 100\%$, $z = 0$ and $w = 0$ in **Figure 1**. It is useful to recognize waste management workers by definition, formal and informal, in daily contact with waste, who are more vulnerable than other categories of the population to potential health problems.

In this way, one of the key issues that is arising all over the world is the need to protect waste workers, formal or informal, as a special asset that provides an essential service. Not only the International Labour Organization, but also many unions and NGOs are advocating putting the protection of waste workers in the center of our attention in this period. For countries outside of the EU and North America, outside of the high-income countries, most recycling is done by independent or informal recyclists who collect materials simply to feed their families [41].

Some countries which have informal recyclers are countries such as South Africa, but also some countries in Europe such as Serbia. There are many people who cannot eat because they are in lockdown. They would normally be picking up recyclables and now they are not allowed to go out. Also people who are in formalized recycling situations. For those in Colombia or Brazil, the government often tells people to stop recycling. At the same time, we even see in the Netherlands a tremendous amount of littering, and so the environment is changing quickly and nobody is really thinking about what these informal workers actually need [61].

Some authors claim that recycling is determined by the country's income level. Low and middle income countries where most recycling happens by independent or informal recyclers, whether formalized as in Brazil and Colombia, or tolerated or semi formalized as in India should have these systems reestablished [62]. What is really important is to figure out a way for them to continue to provide the service that they provide for the city by managing its recyclables and giving the people and their families a way of making a living by thinking actively about how they can safely go about their work [40].

4. Conclusions

We really hope that the post-crisis crisis will be the momentum for radical change in society worldwide. We also propose that people should be referring to expert guidance, not only from their national and regional governments, but also coming out of the World Health Organization and also for low-and middle-income countries.

The COVID-19 crisis assumes that the effects are divided among economic growth, medical and sustainability. So how do we distribute the effect and the recovery efforts between these dimensions? How to allocate time and humans resources, not mention which trials and which patients?

In this chapter we have not wanted to give specialized answers from an economic, or medical or environmental point of view, but rather to relate these answers to other topics of interest to society.

There is an abundance of guidance to discuss about the economy, and to adapt it for the environment, and economically, an austere fiscal policy, which prioritizes employment and reactivation, through the optimization of resources and efforts.

We need to reprioritize our priorities. What is important and what is not important is central, and this is why we also need to face changes in human behavior. We want to argue that one of the things that seem to be a very important thing is the idea of solidarity. It is just a matter of finding it with respect to health care waste because there is a great deal that has been written and it is just necessary that persons access that which it is suitable for the situation. We can build all this knowledge during this new situation, every one of us.

The government response needs to act on three issues. First, to ensure that essential services are carried out without any interruption. Secondly, to ensure worker's safety above any other measure, because we need these teams, we need these people, and we need these heroes on the streets and, thirdly, we need to ensure frequent and easy communication to the citizens to stop fake news and to avoid dissemination of misunderstanding.

Finally, a good way to face the crisis is to win small battles, in health, through the territorial management of contagions, in the environment avoiding very long-term objectives, and instead targeting more short- and medium-term goals.

Author details

Jean Pierre Doussoulin[1,2]

1 Universidad Austral de Chile, Economic Institute, Valdivia, Chile

2 Université Gustave Eiffel, Research Team on the Use of Panel Data in Economics, Paris, France

*Address all correspondence to: jean.doussoulin@uach.cl; jean-pierre.doussoulin@u-pem.fr

References

[1] Klenert D, Funke F, Mattauch L, O'Callaghan B. Five Lessons from COVID-19 for Advancing Climate Change Mitigation. Available SSRN 3622201. 2020;

[2] Wolf LJ, Haddock G, Manstead AS, Maio GR. The importance of (shared) human values for containing the COVID-19 pandemic. Br J Soc Psychol. 2020;59(3):618-27.

[3] Maslow A, Lewis KJ. Maslow's hierarchy of needs. Salenger Inc. 1987;14:987.

[4] Hepburn C, O'Callaghan B, Stern N, Stiglitz J, Zenghelis D. Will COVID-19 fiscal recovery packages accelerate or retard progress on climate change? Oxf Rev Econ Policy. 2020;36.

[5] O'Connell M. To be a machine: adventures among cyborgs, utopians, hackers, and the futurists solving the modest problem of death. Anchor; 2018.

[6] Daly HE. Toward a steady-state economy. Vol. 2. WH Freeman San Francisco; 1973.

[7] Pastén R, Olszynski M, Hantke-Domas M. Does slow and steady win the race? Ecosystem services in Canadian and Chilean environmental law. Ecosyst Serv. 2018;29:240-50.

[8] O'Connor M. Entropy, structure, and organisational change. Ecol Econ. 1991;3(2):95-122.

[9] Doussoulin JP. A paradigm of the circular economy: the end of cheap nature? Energy Ecol Environ. 2020 Oct 1;5(5):359-68.

[10] World Health Organization. Water, sanitation, hygiene and waste management for COVID-19: technical brief, 03 March 2020. World Health Organization; 2020.

[11] Ayres RU. Sustainability economics: Where do we stand? Ecol Econ. 2008;67(2):281-310.

[12] Costanza R, Alperovitz G, Daly H, Farley J, Franco C, Jackson T, et al. Building a sustainable and desirable economy-in-society-in-nature. In: State of the World 2013: Is Sustainability Still Possible? [Internet]. Island Press-Center for Resource Economics; 2014. p. 126-42. Available from: https://www.scopus.com/inward/record.uri?eid=2-s2.0-84893144313&doi=10.5822%2f978-1-61091-458-1_11&partnerID=40&md5=7bc36a99eb3bea4305decf26e24988c4

[13] Morlat C. Sustainable Production System: Eco-development versus Sustainable Development. John Wiley & Sons; 2020.

[14] Korhonen J, Honkasalo A, Seppälä J. Circular Economy: The Concept and its Limitations. Ecol Econ. 2018;143:37-46.

[15] McDonough W, Braungart M. Cradle to cradle: Remaking the way we make things. North point press; 2010.

[16] Esposito M, Tse T, Soufani K. Introducing a Circular Economy: New Thinking with New Managerial and Policy Implications. Calif Manage Rev. 2018;60(3):5-19.

[17] Kirchherr J, Reike D, Hekkert M. Conceptualizing the circular economy: An analysis of 114 definitions. Resour Conserv Recycl. 2017;127:221-32.

[18] de Jesus A, Mendonça S. Lost in Transition? Drivers and Barriers in the Eco-innovation Road to the Circular Economy. Ecol Econ. 2018;145(C):75-89.

[19] Kirchherr J, Piscicelli L, Bour R, Kostense-Smit E, Muller J, Huibrechtse-Truijens A, et al. Barriers to the Circular Economy: Evidence From the European Union (EU). Ecol Econ. 2018;150:264-72.

[20] Cerulli-Harms A, Suter J, Landzaat W, Duke C, Rodriguez Diaz A, Porch L, et al. Behavioural Study on Consumers' Engagement in the Circular Economy. Eur Comm Dir-Gen Justice Consum Bruss Belg. 2018;

[21] Guldmann E. Best Practice Examples of Circular Business Models". Danish Environmental Protection Agency [Internet]. 1st ed. 2016; Available from: https://vbn.aau.dk/en/publications/best-practice-examples-of-circular-business-models

[22] Onoda H. Smart approaches to waste management for post-COVID-19 smart cities in Japan. IET Smart Cities. 2020;2(2):89-94.

[23] Doussoulin JP, Bittencourt M. Analysing the circular economy opportunities in the French construction sector related to the sustainable supply chain: a waste input-output analysis. Int J Supply Chain Oper Resil. 2018;3(2):143-62.

[24] Wu Z, McGoogan JM. Characteristics of and important lessons from the coronavirus disease 2019 (COVID-19) outbreak in China: summary of a report of 72 314 cases from the Chinese Center for Disease Control and Prevention. Jama. 2020;323(13):1239-42.

[25] Kashyap A, Singh K, Sabat D, Maini L. Fast and economic cardboard cutout use to increase compliance of face mask wear during COVID-19 pandemic. J Clin Orthop Trauma. 2020;

[26] Kalina M, Tilley E. "This is our next problem": cleaning up from the covid-19 response. Waste Manag. 2020;

[27] Silva ALP, Prata JC, Walker TR, Duarte AC, Ouyang W, Barcelò D, et al. Increased plastic pollution due to Covid-19 pandemic: challenges and recommendations. Chem Eng J. 2020;126683.

[28] Lancet T. COVID-19: protecting health-care workers. Lancet Lond Engl. 2020;395(10228):922.

[29] Zambrano-Monserrate MA, Ruano MA, Sanchez-Alcalde L. Indirect effects of COVID-19 on the environment. Sci Total Environ. 2020;138813.

[30] Liu K, Wang H, Liu H, Nie S, Du H, Si C. COVID-19: Challenges and perspectives for the pulp and paper industry worldwide. BioResources. 2020;15(3):4638-41.

[31] Sharma HB, Vanapalli KR, Cheela VS, Ranjan VP, Jaglan AK, Dubey B, et al. Challenges, opportunities, and innovations for effective solid waste management during and post COVID-19 pandemic. Resour Conserv Recycl. 2020;162:105052.

[32] Borg G, Giambra S, Knight S. Density and Distancing in the Covid-19 Pandemic. Available SSRN 3597697. 2020;

[33] Razai MS, Doerholt K, Ladhani S, Oakeshott P. Coronavirus disease 2019 (covid-19): a guide for UK GPs. BMJ. 2020;368.

[34] Adams JG, Walls RM. Supporting the health care workforce during the COVID-19 global epidemic. Jama. 2020;323(15):1439-40.

[35] Jamasb T, Nepal R. Issues and options in waste management: A social cost–benefit analysis of waste-to-energy in the UK. Resour Conserv Recycl. 2010;54(12):1341-52.

[36] Hsiang S, Allen D, Annan-Phan S, Bell K, Bolliger I, Chong T, et al. The effect of large-scale anti-contagion policies on the COVID-19 pandemic. Nature. 2020;584(7820):262-7.

[37] Prata JC, Silva AL, Walker TR, Duarte AC, Rocha-Santos T. COVID-19

pandemic repercussions on the use and management of plastics. Environ Sci Technol. 2020;54(13):7760-5.

[38] Klemeš JJ, Van Fan Y, Tan RR, Jiang P. Minimising the present and future plastic waste, energy and environmental footprints related to COVID-19. Renew Sustain Energy Rev. 2020;127:109883.

[39] Guidotti E, Ardia D. COVID-19 data hub. J Open Source Softw. 2020;5(51):2376.

[40] Marinković N, Vitale K, Holcer NJ, Džakula A, Pavić T. Management of hazardous medical waste in Croatia. Waste Manag. 2008;28(6):1049-56.

[41] Baker SR, Bloom N, Davis SJ, Terry SJ. Covid-induced economic uncertainty. National Bureau of Economic Research; 2020.

[42] Lavazza A, Farina M. The Role of Experts in the Covid-19 Pandemic and the Limits of Their Epistemic Authority in Democracy. Front Public Health. 2020;8.

[43] Weible CM, Nohrstedt D, Cairney P, Carter DP, Crow DA, Durnová AP, et al. COVID-19 and the policy sciences: initial reactions and perspectives. Policy Sci. 2020;1-17.

[44] Nzeadibe TC, Ejike-Alieji AU. Solid waste management during Covid-19 pandemic: Policy gaps and prospects for inclusive waste governance in Nigeria. Local Environ. 2020;25(7):527-35.

[45] Vanapalli KR, Sharma HB, Ranjan VP, Samal B, Bhattacharya J, Dubey BK, et al. Challenges and strategies for effective plastic waste management during and post COVID-19 pandemic. Sci Total Environ. 2020;750:141514.

[46] Cook TM. Personal protective equipment during the coronavirus disease (COVID) 2019 pandemic–a narrative review. Anaesthesia. 2020;

[47] Campion N, Thiel CL, Woods NC, Swanzy L, Landis AE, Bilec MM. Sustainable healthcare and environmental life-cycle impacts of disposable supplies: a focus on disposable custom packs. J Clean Prod. 2015;94:46-55.

[48] You S, Sonne C, Ok YS. COVID-19's unsustainable waste management. Science. 2020;368(6498):1438.

[49] Blanco JL, Ambrosioni J, Garcia F, Martínez E, Soriano A, Mallolas J, et al. COVID-19 in patients with HIV: clinical case series. Lancet HIV. 2020;7(5):e314-6.

[50] Ilyas S, Srivastava RR, Kim H. Disinfection technology and strategies for COVID-19 hospital and bio-medical waste management. Sci Total Environ. 2020;749:141652.

[51] Van Fan Y, Jiang P, Hemzal M, Klemeš JJ. An update of COVID-19 influence on waste management. Sci Total Environ. 2020;142014.

[52] Schübeler P, Christen J, Wehrle K. Conceptual framework for municipal solid waste management in low-income countries. Vol. 9. SKAT (Swiss Center for Development Cooperation) St. Gallen; 1996.

[53] Hale T, Petherick A, Phillips T, Webster S. Variation in government responses to COVID-19. Blavatnik Sch Gov Work Pap. 2020;31.

[54] Di Domenico L, Pullano G, Pullano G, Hens N, Colizza V. Expected impact of school closure and telework to mitigate COVID-19 epidemic in France. COVID-19 Outbreak Assess EPIcx Lab. 2020;15.

[55] Farré L, Fawaz Y, González L, Graves J. How the covid-19 lockdown

affected gender inequality in paid and unpaid work in spain. 2020;

[56] Carlsson-Szlezak P, Reeves M, Swartz P. What coronavirus could mean for the global economy. Harv Bus Rev. 2020;3.

[57] Sharma D, Bouchaud J-P, Gualdi S, Tarzia M, Zamponi F. V-, U-, L-or W-shaped recovery after COVID? Insights from an Agent Based Model. Insights Agent Based Model June 15 2020. 2020;

[58] Feng J-C, Tang S, Yu Z. Integrated Development of Economic Growth, Energy Consumption, and Environment Protection from Different Regions: Based on City Level. Energy Procedia. 2019;158:4268-73.

[59] Tesar M. Towards a post-Covid-19 'new normality?': Physical and social distancing, the move to online and higher education. SAGE Publications Sage UK: London, England; 2020.

[60] McKibbin WJ, Fernando R. The global macroeconomic impacts of COVID-19: Seven scenarios. 2020;

[61] World Bank. The economy in the time of COVID-19. Semi-annual report of the Latin America and Caribbean region; April 2020. 2020.

[62] ECLAC. The social challenge in times of COVID-19. 2020;